IN SEARCH OF

INTERCULTURAL UNDERSTANDING

IN SEARCH OF

INTERCULTURAL UNDERSTANDING

A Practical Guidebook for

Living and Working Across Cultures

Third Edition

Patrick L. Schmidt

MERIDIAN WORLD PRESS
Montreal, Canada / Vienna, Austria / Strasbourg, France

Printed in Great Britain

Canadian Cataloging in Publishing Data

Schmidt, Patrick L., 1949-

In Search of Intercultural Understanding – A Practical Guidebook for Living and Working Across Cultures
Includes bibliographical references and index.

ISBN 978-0-9685293-1-7

1. Intercultural studies – Cross-cultural studies. 2. Intercultural communication – Cross-cultural communication

Book cover design by Laurent Michelot and Axel Wendelberger

Quantity discounts are available on bulk purchases of this book for training purposes. For information, contact:

MERIDIAN WORLD PRESS
8, rue Daniel Hirtz
67000 Strasbourg, France
Tel: +33 3 88 44 36 52
Email: patrick.schmidt49@gmail.com

This book is dedicated to my wife

Jacqueline

who provided unfailing support and encouragement

throughout its writing.

ACKNOWLEDGMENTS

This work is the culmination of the many ideas I have acquired while conducting intercultural seminars. These workshops have provided me with the opportunity to bring together and present my thoughts on this subject in a reasonably consistent manner. The questions and comments from my participants caused me to rethink, improve and refine my material and approaches.

As for the theoretical background, I'm most indebted to the writings of Edward and Mildred Hall and Geert Hofstede. Their pioneering concepts have provided frameworks that make the study of culture more comprehensible for students. I would like to especially acknowledge Milton Bennett for his exceptional research on the way the mind adapts to the intercultural experience, as well as his inspiring seminars, which I had the opportunity of attending. And I personally appreciated Nancy Adler's study on how culture impacts business.

Dan MacLeod for his outstanding work on editing the first part of this book, as well as telling me some hard truths on what good writing is. John Lehman and Jürgen Gebhard at the Carl Duisberg Centre for their support and encouragement. Axel Wendelberger for his astute suggestions on layout and artwork and to my nephew, Laurent Michelot, whose French graphic mind provided the final visual touches to this book. Lastly, to Kirti Seetharam, Jenny Flechsenhar, James Chamberlain and Vinita Balasubramanian for their excellent editing and critical remarks.

Contents

PART THREE : Competence

PART FOUR : Global Synergies

PREFACE: THE PARADOX OF KNOWING YOURSELF

Globalization is rapidly breaking down our vision of a world with well-defined national, cultural and linguistic boundaries. Cheap computers and internet service, and innovations like *Google*, *YouTube* and *Wikipedia* are enabling a constant flow of knowledge and ideas across borders. This, along with the emergence of faster and cheaper transportation, has meant even the remotest parts of the planet have been brought into instantaneous contact with one another. Not surprisingly, the study of intercultural communication has taken on an importance that no one could have imagined 15 or 20 years ago.

Still, it is by no means a new field of knowledge. Throughout history people have had contact with others from different cultures, whether through military conquest, missionary religions or commercial trade. The problems caused by cultural differences are well known. Yet, only a minority — diplomats, anthropologists, expatriates, international students — have been traditionally concerned with the issue.

Now we have shifted into a new mode of living where cross-cultural contact has become almost a daily occurrence. Our lives have been enriched, but at the same time become more complex. The very nature of intercultural communication — different languages, behavior patterns and values — makes it imperative to avoid assumptions of similarity, to stimulate consideration of differences.

In Search of Intercultural Understanding attempts to explain those differences and show how to integrate them into your personal and professional endeavors. With the use of illustrations, quotations and exercises, the book presents an easy-to-understand survey of cross-cultural issues. It consciously avoids the wordy, abstract style found all too often in similar publications. Instead, the goal is to sum up the body of professional knowledge so that the average person can grasp the fundamental concepts and apply them to real cross-cultural situations.

The Goal Is Understanding

The fundamental premise of the book is a 3,000-year-old Chinese proverb: "*Those who understand others as well as themselves will be granted success in a thousand encounters.*"

Paradoxically, by studying the codes of another culture and their impact on behavior, you automatically learn more about yourself. This is apparent when you arrive in a foreign country and are confronted by another culture for the first time. Nothing is more startling than realizing how much your work and leisure habits, your taste in food, even your outlook on life continue to depend on values learned in childhood.

The ancient Roman dictum "knowledge is power" becomes relevant here. By learning to be aware of your own cultural baggage, it is possible to transcend your thought-patterns and in the end, be able to comprehend "foreign behavior" more objectively and behave accordingly. You'll make fewer mistakes and the level of goodwill you'll share with your hosts will greatly increase.

To understand your own mental software while simultaneously recognizing that other ways of behaving and thinking are every bit as valid — a sort of "cross-cultural swinging" — is the paradox of knowing yourself. This, in a nutshell, is what real intercultural communication is about.

Using This Guide

This book has been designed for independent study and doesn't assume any previous knowledge on the part of the reader. It is divided into four parts.

First, the concept of culture and its powerful influence on society is explored. Following that is a discussion on the theoretical frameworks designed by social scientists to explain behavioral differences. They will contribute to an initial understanding of how the mind is conditioned in an almost irreversible manner, giving rise to values and beliefs unique to each person's origins. It will become clearer to the reader why cross-cultural interactions are so complex and difficult.

The second part concerns itself with the definition of communication and focuses on the many aspects that cause intercultural interactions to break down: language, non-verbal behavior, perception, stereotypes, ethnocentric attitudes and culture shock. At the end, American, German and Chinese communication patterns are compared.

The third and fourth sections examine strategies and methods to overcome these barriers. We will look at the characteristics of successful diplomats, negotiators and managers and see, in real terms, how intercultural sensitivity is developed and applied.

The objective of *In Search of Intercultural Understanding* is to transport the reader into another mode of thinking through which it becomes possible to creatively examine one's relationship to all cultures, including one's own. The ideas presented in this work should act like an ice-pick, with which you can break down the seas of habit frozen inside your soul and mind.

Some readers may be disappointed that this is not a simple list of *do's and don'ts*. Unfortunately, that is not how good cross-cultural relations work; there is no set script to follow, no magic pill, no "right" answer. Rather, effective intercultural communication is dynamic give-and-take, a sort of "thinking outside the box" phenomenon, where adopting the other person's perspective is of the utmost importance.

Context becomes extremely clear. What may be correct behavior in one situation may be a "don't" in another. Ultimately, intercultural competence is learning and understanding the values and beliefs behind behavior — in short how people think — and reconciling them with your own.

Studying other cultures helps you see yourself as both spectator and participant. At the same time, you gain a frame of reference for your own beliefs and values. This, in the last analysis, is what makes intercultural learning so attractive. If this book encourages the reader to view and analyze cultural differences in terms of "why I act the way I do", it will have succeeded in its mission.

I

Culture

Culture

A Breakdown in Intercultural Communication

Bill Clinton's boots fiasco

In the summer of 1997, *Time* magazine covered the G7 summit near Denver and reported the following:

> "As soon as it happened, the incident became legend. Germans called it 'the boots fiasco.' French commentators sniggered over it. On June 21, as Bill Clinton was playing host to world leaders in Denver, the guests were asked to [dress] themselves for the banquet in jeans, cowboy hats and boots. Though fancy dress was just meant to break the ice, the idea went wrong ... Chancellor Helmut Kohl of Germany, who weighs in in Panzer proportions, balked at the whole rig, but especially the boots. "We had a long discussion about boots, and Kohl said he would never wear them, absolutely never," Italian Prime Minister Romano Prodi said later. President Jacques Chirac of France also refused. A man who very rarely wears jeans, and has never been seen in any kind of hat, Chirac had made a solemn deal with Kohl to stick together on "the [clothing] question."

This story illustrates how people from different countries have their own ways of dealing with day-to-day life. Clinton liked cowboy clothes and, since the summit was being held on a ranch in Colorado, he felt that the other leaders would get a kick out of dressing up as cowboys. He made the mistake of assuming that we all think alike. To his dismay, he found out the others didn't see things the same way. They felt humiliated at the idea.

A classic case of differing perceptions. This minor incident highlights the pitfalls even the best and brightest face when dealing with other cultures. On a more practical level, the breakdown in communication touches on several aspects of relating to others: structure versus informality, decision making, deadlines, relationship building and the purpose of a meeting.

And it raises the broader question of how we really think. The answer to the trap of our "mental software" is to be found through a heightened emphasis on culture-awareness, the interplay of forces that both encourage and discourage understanding between peoples.

Perhaps Bill Clinton might have considered the words of a Chinese emperor before asking his guests to dress like cowboys.

> *The people of the world are bigoted and unenlightened: invariably they regard what is like them as right, and what is different from them as wrong.*
>
> *They do not realize that the types of humanity are not uniform, that it is not only impossible to force people to become different but also impossible to force them to become alike.*
>
> (Yung Cheng 1727)

Questions for reflection

1. Reflect on any experiences of cultural clashes you have had and how you reacted to them.
2. Where did the incident take place?
3. Who was involved?
4. What occurred?
5. To what extent was the incident caused by cultural differences?
6. Have you gained any insights from the event?

The Trap of Similarity

DaimlerChrysler

Their first joint board meeting

The following is a case study of good intentions (and unconscious beliefs in similarity) that led to serious misunderstandings. When Daimler-Benz and Chrysler merged in 1998, the companies decided to hold joint board meetings. Both sides wanted to make a good impression in their first encounter. However each had a radically different idea about what constituted a good presentation.

The Germans began with a long introductory statement — the history of the company, its model range, future prospects —and included lots of background information and hundreds of transparencies. This "train-wreck of a presentation" (as perceived by the Chrysler execs) lasted for almost two hours.

The Americans, on the other hand, presented Chrysler in a simplistic fashion and went straight to their range of models, using showy effects and easy-to-remember slogans. Their approach was like that of an overly-enthusiastic salesman — lots of smiles and jokes — and only 35 minutes long. For the Germans, it was an exercise in superficiality coupled with "optimism gone overboard".

Both sides sincerely believed that they'd done an excellent job but it was apparent the different communication styles weren't working. Chrysler's CEO, Robert Eaton, told a journalist from the *Stuttgarter Zeitung,* "The Germans have a penchant for coming to meetings armed with tons of overhead transparencies and colored charts. It's absolute information overkill."

The Different Meanings of Culture

American participants in intercultural workshops are sometimes surprised to learn that many Europeans perceive Americans as having absolutely no culture. "How could that be?" the startled Americans ask, "We do have culture". An Italian or German might answer, "Our nations have existed much longer than yours, which makes us more refined and mature. You, in the USA, are like undisciplined teenagers — full of energy, but inexperienced and at times dangerously naïve." It's apparent that Americans and Europeans have different ideas on what the term "culture" means.

So before discussing intercultural communication, we need to look at "culture". Webster's New World Dictionary gives different definitions of the word:

1. the cultivation of the soil;
2. development, improvement or refinement of the mind, emotions, interests, manners, tastes;
3. the arts, architecture, political and economic system of a given country — what people create;
4. the attitudes and behavior of a particular social group — how people act.

Many people use the word "culture'" to describe refinement. Others employ it to mean the arts. Although both are perfectly valid, for this book we will use the anthropological approach — how people think and act. To put it more precisely, culture is defined as "the learned and shared values, behaviors and beliefs of a group of interacting people" (Milton Bennett). It is a process of generating and sharing meanings.

This description is often called the subjective approach, the psychological features that define a group. It suggests that the shared set of ideas and practices in people's minds is *socially constructed*. As interculturalist M. Singer puts it, "Culture is essentially *a pattern of learned, group-related perceptions*".

The Chinese say, "Culture is the water we swim in; it surrounds and defines us". This implies a powerful, all-encompassing system where participants don't even realize they're "prisoners" of the patterns surrounding them. The structures provide people with a window through which they view themselves and the world and also serve as a guide to problem-solving and interpreting experiences.

Social scientist Geert Hofstede takes another route to culture by describing it as the "collective programming of the mind". Although some readers might find that his choice of words borders on the more sinister term "brainwashing", it illustrates the process of how values and behaviors are deeply embedded in the human soul.

An example of the "collective programming" process is how the values of individualism and free enterprise are nurtured in the United States. American parents often encourage a 7- or 8-year old child to set up a lemonade stand in front of the house. Children learn to make money through their own initiative and gain early experience in problem-solving. Later on, when interacting with others, they are more likely to exhibit pro-active, "do my own thing" behavior than to seek joint pursuits within a group.

Contrast this with a highly collective culture such as Japan, in which dependence on the group starts in the cradle. A Japanese child is kept close to his parents day and night for two or three years. Interdependent behavior is reinforced in school and later in the workplace. In such an environment, it's natural for people to perceive themselves as a part of "we", which gives us the proverb "the nail that sticks out must be hammered down".

These two opposing thought-patterns are summarized by Alan Roland in his book *In Search of Self in India and Japan*. He psychoanalyzed Americans, Indians and Japanese and found that the two Asian cultures had absolutely no notion of the "inner separation" from others that is so typical of Americans. The author concluded that Americans displayed "a militant individualism, combined with enormous social mobility", permitting very little group identity.

A False Idea:
Culture Means Higher Stages of Civilization

Higher civilization
Civilization
Lower civilization
Higher barbarism
Barbarism
Lower barbarism
Higher savagery
Savagery
Lower savagery

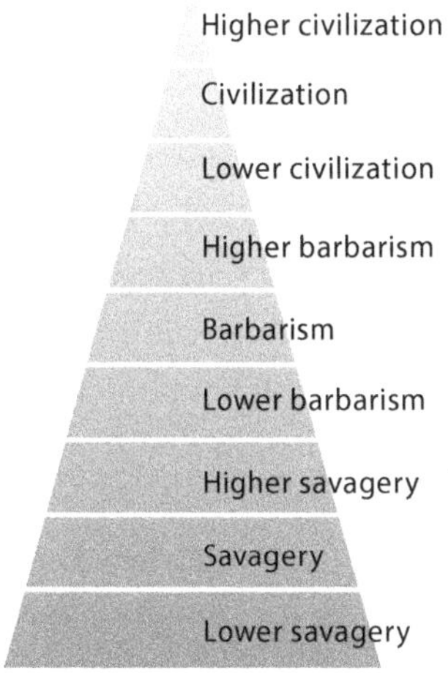

19th century pyramid of human development

Many people in the Western world see themselves as being superior because they feel they have reached the higher stages of human civilization. They point to Third World cultures like those found in the jungles of Asia and Africa. A century ago, it was even rumored that natives walked on all fours, (implying their genetics were closer to the ape than to homo sapiens). Anthropologists remind us that the citizens of so-called "primitive societies" have highly-developed, complex minds and sophisticated social structures.

How is it that some citizens of First World nations persist in believing that certain races are superior to others? This is the definition of "racism" and is contrary to democratic values systems. A bit of history is in order here.

In the second half of the 19th century, it was widely assumed in Europe that only people of European origin possessed culture and had achieved real civilization. Social scientists attempted to apply Darwin's ideas on natural selection to culture. American social scientist Lewis Morgan took the idea and graphically depicted human development as a pyramid with precise definitions for each stage, from "lower savagery" to "higher civilization".

Implicit in this model were notions of hierarchy. At the top were the European colonial powers, the ultimate end-product of civilized development. Those underneath were portrayed either as ignorant barbarians or primitive savages. They were, for the most part, the colonies themselves; small wonder they needed to be "civilized".

It was a highly-respected theory, taught in universities. The butcheries of World War I momentarily suspended its popularity (given the self-inflicted horror Europe had just lived through). Then the Nazis used it as the basis for their claim of German racial superiority. The Holocaust was the direct result of self-definition as the Master Race.

Obviously the idea of a pyramid of human development is preposterous and no social scientist adheres to it. But the reflex is to somehow instinctively believe that it is still present. There is a latent impulse to think that technologically advanced countries are automatically superior to Third World cultures, which we call "primitive".

Other Classifications of Culture

People commonly use "culture" only in terms of national groups such as Russians, French, Brazilians or ethnic groups such as Arab, Latin or Zulu. These larger conglomerations can be viewed on a higher level of abstraction, where general differences in thinking and behavior are found.

However, there are also significant group and individual differences within these national groups that can be observed on a lower level of abstraction. Examples are:

gender: men and women cultures
sexual: heterosexual, homosexual, bisexual
age: seniors, teenagers, etc.
class: working class, middle and upper class
profession: doctors, factory-workers, service-industry employees, etc.
religion: Christianity, Judaism, Islam, Buddhism, Hinduism, etc.
regional: Quebec, Bavaria, Northern Ireland, etc.
company: BMW, Japan Airlines, IKEA etc.

These lower abstract classifications can sometimes prove to be more powerful in holding people together than national culture. For instance, Canadians in French-speaking Quebec often feel more at home with the French in Paris than with their English-speaking compatriots in Toronto.

Corporate culture can also transcend national traits. In 2002 Peugeot and Toyota undertook a joint venture to develop and manufacture the Toyota *Aygo* and Peugeot *107* in Slovakia. Despite their vastly different business experience, not to mention national differences, their shared vision of creating the "best" small car made the adventure a success to the point where it's cited as a model of intercultural cooperation.

OUR CULTURE — OUR TRIBE

A sense of tribe is deeply embedded in the human soul. All of us are appropriately dependent upon and interdependent with networks of belonging. Grounded in the quest for survival and security, millennia of human existence in bands and tribes have fundamentally shaped our attitudes and behaviors as a species... So we use the word "tribe" with caution, as a metaphor to acknowledge an aspect of human evolution at the core of our social identity. Our prosperity as social beings is woven by patterns of kinship, mutual assistance and affection.

Despite individualism's triumph, the Industrial Revolution, the power of Nation States and international corporations, nothing has finally erased the human need to belong, to share an identity with others whom we recognize as "like me" and "one of us."

Source: L. Daloz *Common Fire: Lives of Commitment in a Complex World*

The gathering of a group of interacting people with shared values and behaviors — the tribal feeling — is the central theme of Rembrandt's compelling The Nightwatch.

Socialization: The Process of Acquiring Culture

In 1940, 17-year-old Heinz Grunwald arrived in New York City as a Jewish refugee from Vienna. He quickly changed his name to "Henry," mastered English, and ended up as a copy boy's job at *Time* magazine. From then on his life evolved around American journalism, ending up as editor-in-chief of *Time* for almost 30 years. In his autobiography *One Man's America*, he described how he enthusiastically adopted his new country, but pointed out how his behavior was continually influenced by his early experiences in Austria.

What he was referring to was the socialization process we all go through in the first years of our life. We learn "correct behavior", i.e. patterns of thinking, from our families, friends, schools, religious institutions and even from TV commercials. This cultural conditioning is most powerful in the first ten to twelve years of life, when most of our effort goes toward learning about the world in which we find ourselves, assimilating values and behavioral patterns.

According to neuropsychologists, these "conditioned responses" are not only natural but are etched into our nervous systems. Despite the recently discovered neuroplasticity of the brain, these responses become part of our personality. Just as you "burn" information onto a CD, the process which takes place in the nervous system cannot be completely erased. Given the almost irreversible learning patterns of early childhood, it's extremely difficult to take on a new culture.

Although a 60-year-old Austrian-American may have arrived in New York at the age of 17, there will always be social reflexes and non-verbal behavior to remind both the person in question and his friends that he was not, in fact, "born in the U.S.A.".

As the socialization process is, for the most part, not explicit, attempting to grasp and articulate one's own cultural values is a formidable task. This is because patterns are so well ingrained in our minds and nervous systems that we can't imagine being otherwise. When we're asked to identify our feelings, we find it difficult to express specifics. Our reactions are tightly woven into all parts of our personality and control our thoughts. Lifestyle, speech, how we behave toward one another...

"Culture hides more than it reveals and, strangely enough, what it hides, it hides most effectively from its own participants." so says American anthropologist Edward Hall.

Examples of Socialization

Learning how to behave in one's own culture takes place in many settings. When American children attend elementary school, for example, they are repeatedly told, "Any one of you can become President of the United States; it's up to you!". The ideal of becoming anything you want explains in part the highly-optimistic trait of believing in oneself "against all odds". For Americans it's normal to think this way, just common sense. Most of the world would strongly disagree.

It comes as a complete surprise to most Americans that their optimistic view is not shared by everyone, regardless of country or culture. Yet, if you were to ask the people of India whether they'd ever considered they might be Prime Minister one day, you'd get nearly a billion *Nos*. Indians are strongly influenced both by acceptance (or fatalism from the Western perspective) and "karma". If you succeed, so much the better — your present life was destined to be successful. If you fail, destiny was unkind — maybe in another life things will turn out differently.

Television has become as powerful an instrument as school. It overwhelms us with images and sound and stories with lessons loosely attached. If you believe what you see on TV, most Americans live upper-middle class lives, as depicted in "Desperate Housewives".

"Language does serve as a tool for communication, but in addition, it is a 'system of representation' for perception and thinking."
— Milton Bennett

Television is an extension of the Silver Screen and movies have been sending powerful messages to viewers everywhere for a century. In an extreme example, there was the German exchange student arriving at an American high school who was greeted with a "*Heil Hitler*" salute by a girl, who had seen it in war films and "thought that's how Germans greeted each other."

Whether via family, school or media, the acquisition of language is your window to the world. Most people underestimate the pervasive power one's native tongue has in the socialization process. Your language translates internalized thought, through which you embody the "mentality", the shared perceptions of a culture. Our language habits predispose and nudge us gently to certain patterns of meaning. And, obviously, our thinking is affected by the words which are available in our given language.

For example, Germans firmly believe that putting verbs at the end of sentences and clauses makes for a disciplined, no-nonsense entity. And it requires the listener to pay attention until the end in order to fully understand what's been said. Consider the following:

> *Die Hauptbotschaft, die ich Ihnen vermittln möchte, lautet, dass das Lernen sowie das Verständnis von interkulturellen Unterschieden entscheidend zu dem Erfolg von Geschäftsbeziehungen im Ausland beitragen können.*
> Translated: The main message, that I you transmit would like, states, that the learning as well as the understanding of intercultural differences decisively to the success of business relations abroad contribute can.

For non-German speakers, putting compound verbs at the end of the sentence, as well as packing subordinate phrases inside, is most unnatural and cumbersome.

Compare the thought-patterns of an American, whose language tends to be playful and opportunistic, placing emphasis on movement. If the above-mentioned German sentence were to be expressed by an American, it would be far more telegraphic. "Look, if you want to get along and make deals in some foreign country, you got to know how the folks think."

Another problem is that of experimental equivalence. Objects or experiences that are idiomatic to one people may not translate into the language of another. Each culture has unique expressions which verbalize their perception of the world and the "feel" of the words can never be satisfactorily captured.

savoir vivre (the art of living) from France,
guanxi (linking of two people in mutual dependence) from China,
Ordnung muß sein (there must be order) from Germany,
time is money from the USA,
machismo (concern for status and appearances) from Mexico
budi (respect, courtesy and gentleness toward others) from Malaysia.

These expressions structure thought and behavior in subtle ways, not consciously apparent to those using them. The linguist Benjamin Whorf summed it up by stating that the language we speak is largely interrelated with the way we think which, in turn, strongly influences how we understand reality and dictates how we behave.

Learning to write your language can affect cognitive style. Children in Japan and China spend years practicing between two to eight thousand complex calligraphic characters. Not only is the meaning conveyed but, equally important, the visual aspect of the written characters is assimilated. Consequently Japanese and Chinese people become more sensitive to visual and spatial qualities.

Note the Japanese tea ceremony and the importance of arranging food in an aesthetic manner. And it's no accident that *Feng Shui* — the harmonious arrangement of space — is highly valued by both countries.

After World War II, Taiwan and Japan kick-started their economies by becoming excellent copiers of Western products and technology. Today, Japan and China, while having diversified their economies, continue to use this cultural sense of detailed observation in their manufacturing processes.

Chinese and Japanese children focus much attention on the aesthetic value of calligraphic characters when learning to write, which in turn makes their orientation to visual sensations more pronounced in adult life.

When all is said and done, mental constructs are primarily based on our mother tongue, making it hard to change attitudes and adopt new approaches. Our filtered perceptions are a powerful psychological obstacle to our ability to interpret other cultures. Although learning a second language to the point of fluency can help enormously, we will never instinctively "think" like a native-speaker. And, if we aren't consciously aware of how much language influences thought-patterns, we will have a much more difficult time. As the American communications-researcher Winston Brembeck once said, "To know another's language and not its culture is a very good way to make a fluent fool of oneself."

Hofstede's Pyramid of Human Uniqueness

Using the model of a pyramid, Geert Hofstede illustrated the "three levels of uniqueness in human mental programming". He attempts to display how every person is in some way like all other people, then some, then none. When trying to comprehend the socialization process, it helps to take all these levels into consideration.

The bottom part represents the traits we all share, mental programming inherited from our genes. It corresponds to our need to eat, sleep and survive; our

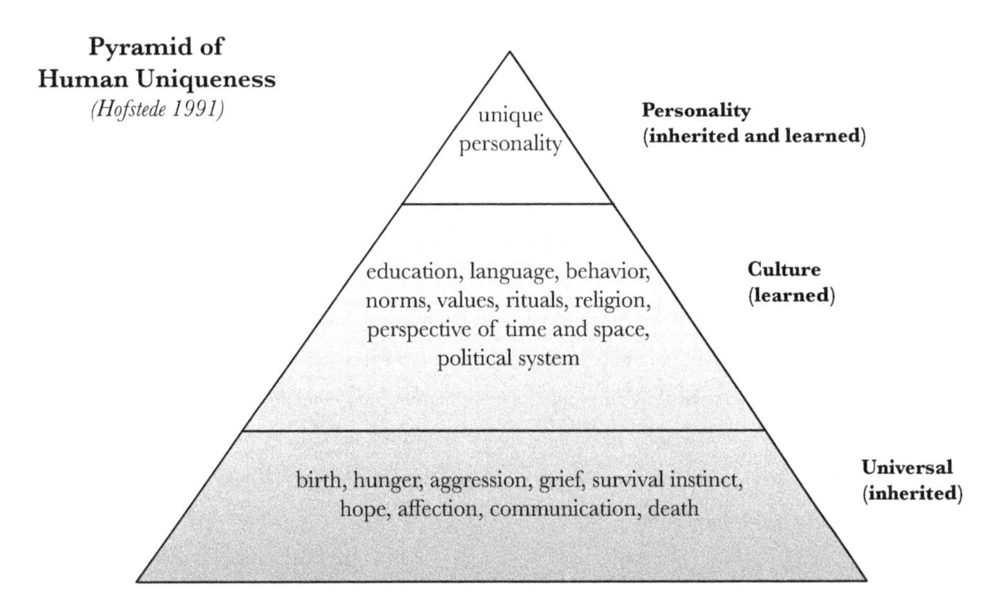

ability to feel anger, fear, love and sadness; to observe the outside world and talk about it with other people.

How we go about expressing these characteristics depends on the middle part — culture. Our behavior is learned through socialization by the particular group of people who surround us.

The personality of the individual is his or her unique mental program, a combination of genes and the personal experiences he or she has acquired.

Still, our national culture usually imposes itself on our universal traits, modifying them to the point where we become an overly-polite Japanese, an animated Italian, a sunny-boy American, a serious German and so on...

Questions for reflection

Think about your own culture.
How did the socialization process take place in your own life?
Try to recall some of the behavior and values you were taught early in life.
How do they affect you now?
And the use of language — are you aware of its power to indirectly determine behavior (via perception and expression)?
Can you cite examples of everyday language that might affect your mental patterns?

> "What I say is this, and this I do not say to all Englishmen. God made us different, you and I, and your fathers and my fathers. For one thing, we have not the same notions of honesty and speaking the truth. That is not our fault, because we are made so. And look now what you do. You come and judge us by your own standards of morality. You are, of course, too hard on us. And again I tell you, you are great fools in this matter: Who are we to have your morals, or you to have ours?"
>
> – Rudyard Kipling, *East and West*

UNIVERSAL, CULTURAL, OR PERSONAL TRAITS

At the beginning of each sentence, put a "U" if you think the behavior is universal, "C" if it is cultural, or "P" if it is personal.

1. __Going to a job interview unshaved.
2. __Wearing a bathing suit when entering a church.
3. __Considering leeches to be good for curing blood-related diseases.
4. __ Running away from a lion.
5. __Enjoying tacos with spicy sauce.
6. __Sleeping
7. __ Sleeping in the nude.
8. __Preferring playing poker to doing homework.
9. __Dressing up for a job interview.
10. __Being wary of going into a deep, dark cave.
11. __Calling your secretary "love".
12. __Regretting having lost the family fortune.
13. __Saying "Excuse me" after inadvertently bumping into someone.
14. __Showing respect to a police officer.
15. __Feeling sad at the death of your father.

(For suggested answers, see page 137)

Understanding Culture through Metaphors

The best way to understand culture is to examine it through metaphors. Culture is what water is to a fish. The fish takes water for granted. Remove it from its environment and the fish realizes it needs water to survive.

The same applies to us. We're not aware of our own culture until we're outside of it. Only when we bump into new surroundings do we realize that our basic values and assumptions aren't universal. This is when we spontaneously say to ourselves, "I feel like a fish out of water".

The most commonly used metaphor for culture is the iceberg. Its tip corresponds to our first contact with a new culture, such as:

historical monuments — the Tour Eiffel in France, Taj Mahal in India
dress customs — Lederhosen in southern Germany, Swiss Guards in the Vatican
speaking habits — British understatement, the politeness of Japanese
non-verbal behavior — vodka glasses thrown over shoulders in Russia
food — *couscous* in Tunisia, *dim sum* in Hong Kong
rituals — kissing of cheeks in France, bowing to a superior in Japan

These visible parts are commonly referred to as *objective culture* and they're our opinion from Day One. Unless we know the invisible values, attitudes and traditions, there's little chance we'll understand what's happening (even though it's observable). And there's a real risk of stereotyping and forming prejudices. (Italy is a land of spaghetti-eaters, the U.S.A. is a nation of cowboys, Argentina is the country of tango dancers).

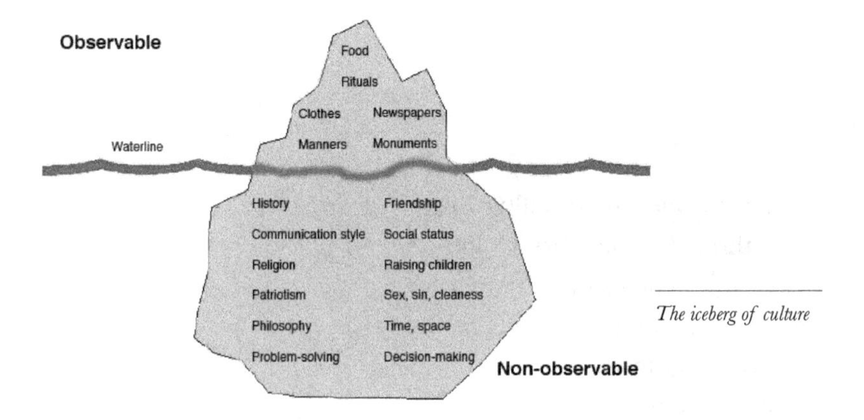

The iceberg of culture

To generate real intercultural communication, you need to go below the water level. The non-observable part of the iceberg is known as *subjective culture.* This is where unspoken assumptions are found, the core values and patterns that guide our thoughts and actions. Some cultures value individualism, others prefer collective orientation. Some cultures build relationships as a pre-requisite to accomplishing tasks, others build relationships after the work is done. Some cultures are comfortable moving quickly and taking risks; others choose to go slowly and look at all the information before taking the first step. All behavior provides us with insights on how cultures "tick". The extent to which you are conscious of different values and communication styles will determine your success (or lack thereof) in a foreign country.

> "Culture hides more than it reveals and, strangely enough, what it hides, it hides most effectively from its own participants.
>
> Years of study have convinced me that the real job is not to understand foreign culture but to understand our own."
>
> — Edward Hall

To see how strongly "invisible" values influence decision-making, take a look at the moral dilemma on the next page. It was posed by Samuel Stouffer, an American sociologist, back in 1951 (further developed by the management research team of Fons Trompenaars and Charles Hampden-Turner). It comes down to a basic, and difficult, choice: do you adhere to legal rules — in this case, the law against perjury — or ignore your own society's values in favor of loyalty to a friend or relative?

A DILEMMA

To lie or not to lie — that is the question

You are riding in a car driven by your best friend in a zone where the speed limit is 40 km per hour. You notice he's going at least 20 km per hour too fast. Although you warn him, he doesn't slow down. Suddenly he hits — and kills — a pedestrian. You are the only witness.

Your friend's lawyer says he probably won't go to jail if you testify that the car was traveling at normal speed.

1. What would you do?

   a. As my friend, he has a right to expect me to testify in his favor and I will.

   b. He has no right to expect me to lie for him and I won't.

2. How do you think citizens of the following nations would choose (in terms of percentage of population)?

   Holland

   Great Britain

   Singapore

   Greece

   Venezuela

   USA

   France

   Germany

   South Korea

   (answers on next page)

Exercise

	a) % who would lie	b) % who would not lie*
Holland	10	90
Great Britain	9	91
Singapore	31	69
Greece	39	61
Venezuela	68	32
USA	7	93
France	27	73
Germany	13	87
South Korea	63	37

(Source: Trompenaars and Hampden-Turner 1997)

People in Venezuela, South Korea and Greece are far more likely to lie to the police than in Northern Europe and America, where rules are seen to be more important than friends. Interculturalist Trompenaars calls the two groups "particularists" and "universalists".

A particularist will say, "how can you trust people who won't even protect their best friends?" On the other hand, the universalist can't understand how anyone can ignore the common good in favor of a criminal, no matter who he or she is.

What Can We Conclude From This Cross-Cultural Dilemma?

1. There are no right or wrong solutions; persons from different cultures perceive and organize their environment in different ways so that it becomes meaningful to them. If you understand the principle that values are relative, then you are on your way to becoming interculturally competent. You're beginning to tolerate ambiguity and becoming non-judgmental.

2. To be an effective and interculturally competent person, you must be able to put yourself in other people's shoes. The ability to understand and share their inner logic, known as empathy, is the key to good relations. However, this doesn't mean you have to accept the other culture's point of view, much less adopt it.

*It should be noted these results indicate how people responded to the questionnaire and doesn't necessarily mean that they would do the same in an actual courtroom. Nevertheless, the differing percentages make us aware of the extent to which culture influences decision-making.

VALUES AND BEHAVIOR

As with the iceberg metaphor, we see how certain aspects of culture are visible — they appear in people's behavior — while others remain hidden in the sphere of thinking, feeling, believing.

The exercise below demonstrates how observable behavior is related to unseen values. Match the value or belief in the column on the left to its manifestation in the column on the right.

1. Informality	___Expressing your disappointment through irony, satire.
2. Egalitarianism	___Arriving at a meeting without a tie.
3. Relying on only oneself	___Taking time off work to visit your mother in the hospital.
4. Respect for age	___ Refusing to help the student next to you during an exam.
5. Honesty	___ At a meeting , openly telling your boss he's wrong.
6. Directness	___ Listening to an older person even though you're not interested.
7. Respect for authority	___In court, telling the truth under oath.
8. Indirectness	___Letting interns give their opinions on sales figures.
9. Fatalism	___Asking the engineer's opinion of something he's an expert on.
10. Importance of family	___Submissively accepting that some events in life are pre-determined.

(Suggested answers on page 137)

Cultural Frameworks

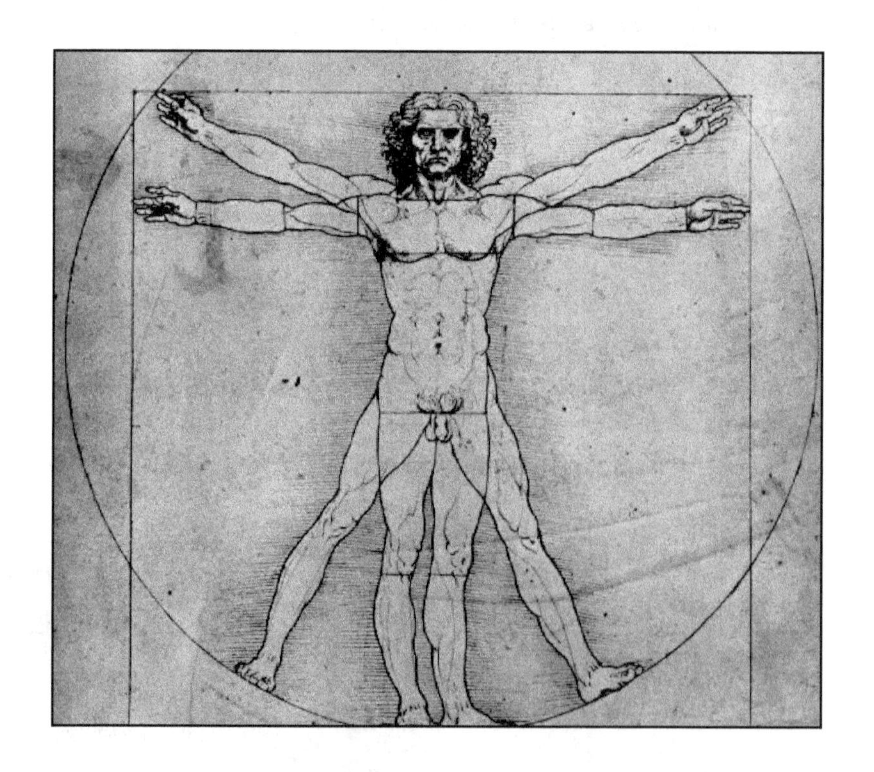

Explaining why people act the way they do.

Social researchers have arrived at quite a few theories to explain why people from different countries do things in different ways. But just what ***is*** a theory anyway?

In the dictionary it's defined as: an *approximate* explanation of why something is the way it is. The theoretical is never exact, nor certain.

Even if our opinions on people's behavior are more emotional, theories on culture are no different. All they can do is frame what behavioral tendencies we might expect in a given society. They are tools, nothing more: practical methods for "reading" cultural patterns as far as such a thing is even possible!

The picture we carry in our minds looks something like this:

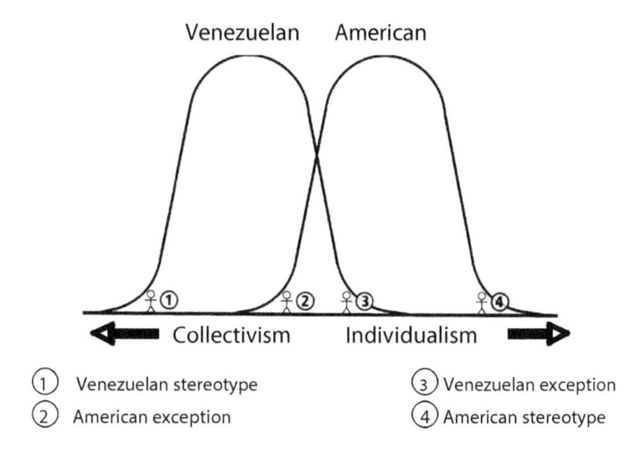

Venezuelans are more collective and Americans more individualistic in general. But obviously, there are Venezuelans who are every bit as individualistic as any American and vice-versa. The individuals who overlap are actually *deviants* in terms of the norm.

Geert Hofstede and Edward Hall propose frameworks which form the base of contemporary intercultural studies. They provide us with alternative lenses through which to view and appreciate cultures in general.

HOFSTEDE'S DIMENSIONS OF WORK-RELATED VALUES

Geert Hofstede's impressive studies of values in the workplace offer one approach to understanding the power of our upbringing and environment. His premise is that people carry mental programs developed during childhood and reinforced by their surroundings throughout their lives.

From 1967 to 1973, while working at IBM as a social scientist, he collected data from more than 116,000 IBM employees worldwide and at all levels, from the unskilled worker to the chief executive officer. Because they all worked for the same company and because characteristics such as age, gender and job-category were matched, the differences in their professional habits could mainly be attributed to national culture. By using average scores for each country, Hofstede was able to generate profiles that explained the differences.

In 1980, he developed a model that identified four primary dimensions in differentiating cultures:

- individualism-collectivism
- power distance
- uncertainty avoidance
- masculinity-femininity

Later he added a fifth dimension — short- and long-term orientation.

His work is important because it represents the best attempt at empirically measuring differences in values worldwide. Despite some criticism — information was collected mostly from males and it under-represented certain parts of the planet (Africa and the former Soviet bloc) — his findings have remained important across time.

Individualism-Collectivism

Critical incident

What do you think is happening here?

A self-employed American consultant is seeking to expand business in Germany. He makes a series of presentations and is inevitably asked which consulting group he works for. He doesn't know how to react; he's never been asked this in the United States. He explains his status but feels as if he should almost apologize.

Commentary

Germany, compared to the U.S., is more a collective society and values belonging to a group and consensual decision-making. As members of a "we" society, where commitment and loyalty are key values, Germans unconsciously project their values onto the American; they're uncomfortable at his "lone wolf" profile.

Individualistic cultures stress self-actualization. It's a "me" society, where autonomy is paramount. People are expected to look after themselves and, at best, their immediate families. They tend to distance themselves from each other both psychologically and emotionally. They are self-starters, who see "challenges" where others might see problems.

The American consultant believes in self-reliance, in taking the initiative and looking after his own interests. Personal achievement is preferred to loyalty. "The squeaky wheel gets the grease" says it all.

> "People in an individualist culture feel a need to communicate verbally when meeting people. Silence is considered abnormal. In a collectivist culture just being together is emotionally sufficient; there is no compulsion to talk."
> — Geert Hofstede

Hofstede summarized the collectivist-individualist dimension as follows:

Collectivist	**Individualistic**
Identity based on group	Identity based on self
'We" society	"Me" society
Harmony important	Honesty important
Relationship-oriented	Task-oriented
Organizations, clubs, networks	Individual achievement
Group management	Management of individuals

The scale below indicates how some countries differ in collectivism-individualism.

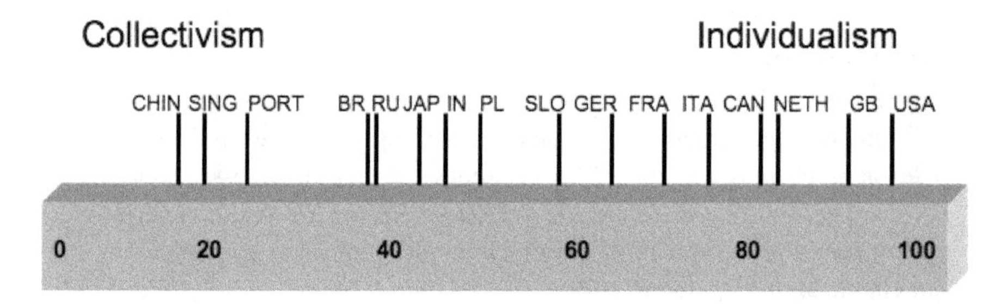

Country abbreviations: Kor - Korea, Sing - Singapore, Port - Portugal, Gre - Greece, Jap - Japan, Pl - Poland, Slo - Slovenia, Ger - Germany, Fra - France, Ita - Italy, Can - Canada, Neth - Netherlands, GB - Great Britain, USA - United States of America, Swe - Sweden, Spa - Spain, CH - Switzerland, In - India, Chin - China, RU - Russia, BR - Brazil

The Ideal American Individualist

American heroes are loners, portrayed by such actors as John Wayne and Clint Eastwood. They are strong, independent people who struggle to shape their own destinies and won't take "no" for an answer. In business circles, American self-image seeks to combine the rugged spirit of the pioneers with adventurous entrepreneurship.

John Wayne, the classic American hero of strong individualism

INDIVIDUALISTIC or COLLECTIVIST

Go through the sentences below and decide which apply to people in an individualistic culture/collectivist culture:

1. __People respect and uphold traditions.
2. __ People receive bonuses based on sales.
3. __ Interdepartmental rivalry is strong.
4. __ Employee-of-the-month certificates are offered.
5. __ Over a dozen clauses and amendments are part of a standard sales contract.

6. __ People change the company they work for every three years on average.
7. __ It 's best to let out your feelings and clear the air.
8. __ People dream of being stars — uniquely successful.
9. __ It's most important to save face in all situations.
10. __ Mothers ask their two-year-olds what they want to eat.
11. __ Self-help books are bestsellers.
12. __ Consensus between industry, unions and the state is normal.
13. __ Marriages are arranged by the family.
14. __ Opinions are decided by the group.
15. __ People go to "pot-luck" dinner parties where everyone brings part of the meal.

(For suggested answers, see page 137)

Power Distance

Critical incident

What do you think is happening here?

> Back in 1809 Sweden had a problem. King Gustav IV was so incompetent that Parliament had him removed and began looking for an outside candidate to take over. Someone suggested one of Napoleon's generals, Jean-Baptiste Bernadotte, a brilliant strategist who enjoyed the privileges of power.
>
> Upon being crowned, Bernadotte addressed Parliament in Swedish. Unfortunately, his command of the language was lamentable; some members laughed out loud. The new king was so upset he never spoke a word of Swedish again. Despite this, he ruled for the next 35 years and was adored by the Swedish people.

Commentary

Sweden has always been an egalitarian society whose citizens don't bow to authority or class privilege. Status and titles are far less important than competence. Not so in France, where inequalities are seen as a fact of life. Class distinctions are ingrained and hierarchy is not questioned.

Jean-Baptiste Bernadotte expected to be respected unconditionally because he was accorded authority and was addressing subordinates. His French upbringing didn't prepare him to be laughed at and disrespected by the inferior classes.

Hofstede defines power distance as "the extent to which the less powerful members of institutions and organizations within a country expect and accept that power is distributed unequally." In countries such as Sweden, the Netherlands and the US, it's considered perfectly okay to do a job without consulting the boss. Not so in countries such as India, France and Singapore where not consulting management before making a decision is considered insubordination.

In other words, do you work in a particular way because your boss tells you to (high power distance) or are you relatively autonomous (low).

Power Distance

Low	**High**
Uncomfortable with inequalities	Inequalities expected
Boss is a "resourceful democrat"	Boss is autocratic and paternalistic
Staff expects to be consulted (flat hierarchy)	Staff expects to be told what to do (steep hierarchy)
Privileges and status symbols frowned upon	Privileges and status symbols popular
Students treat teachers as equals	Formal student-teacher relationship
Subordinates rewarded for taking initiative	Subordinates closely supervised

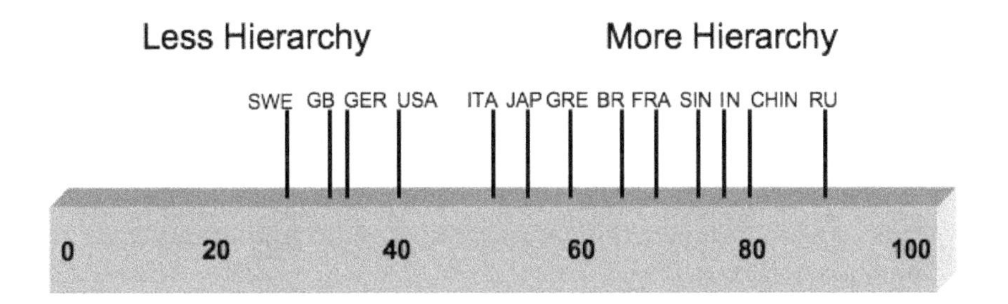

CASE STUDY

A Swede in Paris

Carl, a Swedish employee working for a French company, was frustrated at the time it took for decisions to be made between departments. He was used to making decisions himself. Although he'd been instructed to go through certain channels, he decided to fax his proposals directly to a counterpart in another department.

The head of Carl's department was extremely upset. He called him in and told him in no uncertain terms that every fax had to be approved before being sent.

Uncertainty Avoidance

Critical incident

What do you think is happening here?

> "What strikes a foreigner traveling in Germany is the importance attached to the idea of punctuality, whether or not the standard is realized. Punctuality, not the weather, is the standard topic of conversation for strangers in railway compartments. Long distance trains in Germany have a pamphlet laid out in each compartment called a *Zugbegleiter*, which lists all the stops with arrival and departure times and all the possible connections en route. It is almost a national sport in Germany, as a train pulls into a station, for hands to reach out for the *Zugbegleiter* so that the train's progress may be checked against the digital watch. When trains are late, and it happens, the loudspeakers relay this fact in a tone which falls between the stoic and the tragic. The worst category of lateness, which figures in these announcements, is *unbestimmte Verspätung* (indeterminable lateness: we don't know how late it is going to be!) and this is pronounced as a funeral oration." — Peter Laurence, British sociologist.

Commentary

This incident demonstrates how one culture deals with uncertainty. The future may be unpredictable but how we face the unknown is subjective, learned behavior.

Hofstede refers to this as the uncertainty avoidance dimension. In countries such as Germany, where people are especially averse to uncertainty, security is sought through an extensive set of rules and thorough training. The more structure there is, the better. Experts are highly respected and their knowledge seldom questioned. When a project is undertaken, it's thoroughly researched beforehand.

Cultures with low uncertainty avoidance, such as Great Britain, tend to be more flexible. People are far less afraid to take risks. Unconventional behavior is not seen as threatening; in fact, eccentrics are often admired. Generalists are preferred to specialists and common sense is the law.

Uncertainty Avoidance

Low	**High**
Uncertainty is a part of life	Order is a must (*Ordnung muß sein*)
Unstructured situations are okay	The more structure, the better
Disagreeing is normal	Strong need for consensus
Risk-taking is good	Chance is kept to a minimum
As few rules as possible	Need for written rules
Generalists / common sense	Experts / specialized knowledge

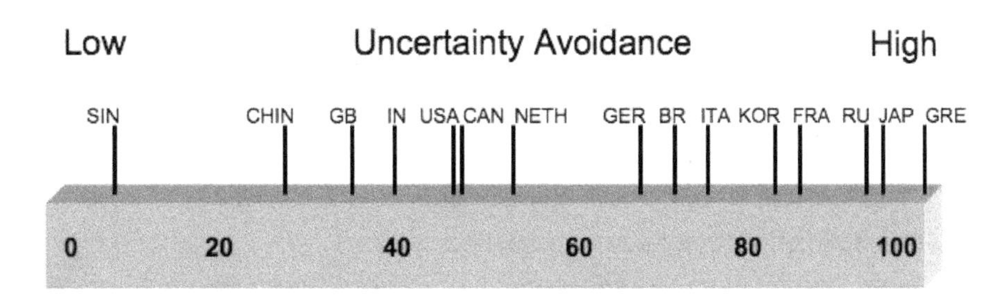

Interpreting History through Cultural Values

The high need for structure and thorough training shaped German combat strategy during World War II. In *The Rise and Fall of the Great Powers*, Paul Kennedy claims a major reason the German army was able to hold out for so long during the last months of the war was the relative independence and extraordinarily high level of training among staff officers and the non-commissioned officers. Their thorough preparation allowed the army to implement an operational doctrine, known as the *Innere Führung* (internal leadership) principle, that "emphasized flexibility and decentralized decision-making at the battlefield level, which proved far superior to the enthusiastic but unprofessional forward rushes of the Allied forces".

Case Study

Japanese Need for Thoroughness and Structure

Michael Hill and George Brown are American engineers working in their company's subsidiary in Tokyo. They were recently assigned to help two Japanese engineers choose a new software program.

Both Michael and George felt their colleagues were asking too many basic questions and wasting everybody's time by spinning out hypothetical situations. They decided to make a show of American pragmatism and reached a deal with a software company after only two days.

Their hosts were pleasantly surprised by such quick results and, although they'd wanted to look at alternatives, they approved the purchase.

A few days after the software was introduced, it became clear there were severe compatibility problems. The program was withdrawn and the team had to start all over again.

What happened here?

Americans typically take the approach, "Let's try this out and, if it doesn't work, we'll try something else". They know that things are rarely perfect — mistakes happen — and life is inherently unpredictable. Pragmatism is the answer. Michael and George applied the trial-and-error methodology, reflecting the American tolerance for uncertainty, thus confirming Hofstede's research.

From the Japanese point of view, the Americans didn't collect enough information and took an unnecessary risk. They should have made more of an effort to analyze and evaluate alternatives; in the end, everyone lost time and money. But Americans move quickly once they think they have a viable solution.

HIGH OR LOW UNCERTAINTY AVOIDANCE

For each of the statements below, mark "H" if you think it shows high uncertainty avoidance and "L" when it's the opposite.

1. __ We've got to get this right the first time or we're finished.

2. __ Well, let's just agree to disagree; there's room for more than one approach.

3. __ We need to spell things out clearly: who's responsible if this goes wrong?

4. __ Janet doesn't like to stay in one place — she changes jobs at least once a year.

5. __ Pierre always keeps his emotions under control.

6. __ You never know when Jürgen is going to blow up.

7. __ The Board of Directors insists that we bring in experts to make sure we've made the right decision.

8. __ A people that elects a former body-builder and movie star as their governor isn't too worried about risks.

9. __ Students expect teachers to be experts in their field of study.

10. __Watanabe was made department head because he's the best at what we do.

11. __The company doesn't like executives who are overly willing to bend the rules.

12. __Mark is our most creative person; the trouble is he always forgets his appointments.

13. __The British have great admiration for eccentric people.

14. __I make good common sense decisions — I don't need an expert to tell me how to act.

15. __ Susan always has a neat desk, never a pencil out of place.

(Suggested answers on page 137)

Masculinity - Femininity

Critical incident

What do you think is happening here?

> A few years back, an unusual Formula 1 race took place in Spain. Mika Hakkinen was leading by over 40 seconds with less than a lap to go. In the broadcast booth, they were already celebrating the Finn's victory when his engine blew up 400 meters from the finish line. Hakkinen got out of the car, took off his helmet and stared at the smoking engine. To their astonishment, the television audience saw tears rolling down his cheeks.

Commentary

According to Hofstede all cultures balance masculine values of achievement and assertiveness against nurturing and social support, seen as feminine ones. Japan, Mexico, Germany and the US are regarded as masculine societies and respect "tough" symbols like money, success and fearlessness. People are judged on their professional status and the material goods they've managed to acquire. Teachers praise their best students because performance is the key to success. Finally, an open display of emotions — especially crying — is seen as unmanly.

A "feminine" culture puts emphasis on tender values such as care for others, quality of life and relationships in general. Teachers don't often praise individual achievements because social adjustment is regarded as more important. Students are more likely to cooperate with one another and develop a sense of solidarity; modesty and friendliness are more important than brilliance. Men's and women's roles are less distinct and often equal. The Scandinavian countries score high in feminine values by emphasizing a friendly environment, job security and group decision-making. And men are allowed to cry.

Feminine	**Masculine**
Quality of life in the workplace	Performance
Caring for others	Looking out for Nr. 1
Need for consensus / harmony	Need to compete / win
Empathy with the unfortunate	Admiration for winners
Modesty	Overconfidence

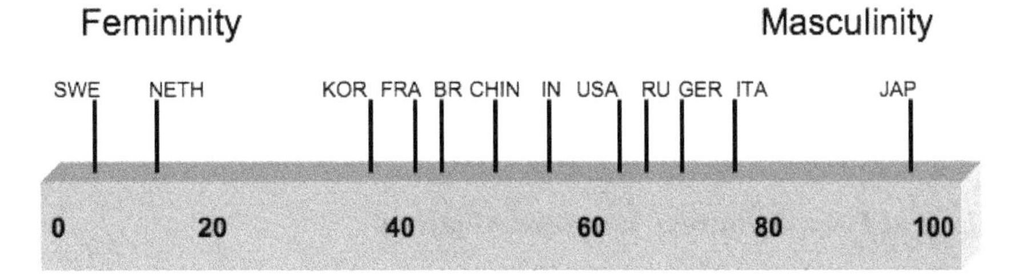

Child Welfare in Rich Countries

A UNICEF "Report Card: Child Poverty in Perspective", released in early 2007, rated the well-being of children in 21 industrialized countries. It ranked countries according to how they scored in six categories: material wealth, health and safety, education, peer- and family- relationships, risk behavior and the children's own sense of well-being.

It's interesting to look at this study from the perspective of Hofstede's four dimensions. The four highest-ranked countries — the Netherlands, Sweden, Denmark and Finland —are the same ones which received the highest "feminine" scores.

The US and the UK, countries that scored very high in masculinity and highest in individualism, were at the very bottom of the list, twentieth and twenty-first respectively. Their poor results were attributed to economic inequalities and a lack of public support for families, social issues that play a small role in individualistic and masculine cultures.

EDWARD HALL'S CULTURAL FRAMEWORKS

Edward Hall, considered to be the Godfather of intercultural studies, has written extensively about the relationship between culture and communication. His books, *The Silent Language* (1959), *The Hidden Dimension* (1966) and *Understanding Culture Differences* (1990) are well known. Hall examines the way people talk to one another in a given society. His conclusion: context is everything. "The information that surrounds an event [...] is inextricably bound up with the meaning of that event."

High- and Low-Context Communication

Critical incident

What do you think is happening here?

> Marie is a young French woman, living with her Swiss-German boyfriend in Zurich. One day she buys a sweater, brings it home and asks Peter how she looks in it. He doesn't like it at all and he says so, going so far as to use the word "horrible".
> Surprised by his lack of tact, Marie says he's not acting like a very nice person. Peter is taken aback; what should he have said?
> "At the very least, you could have said the pattern was nice!"
> Peter can't believe what he's hearing and gives her a cursory glance.
> "But why should I say what I don't think?"
> "Because I thought you loved me!"

Commentary

This is a clash between direct and indirect communication. Hall worked out ground-breaking concepts about the different ways we express our experiences to the people who surround us. He classifies societies according to a scale of low- and high-context. High-context communication is implicit: coded, circular, indirect. Marie's message comes not only through words, but through non-verbal language and her relationship with Peter.

This can be experienced in international business. For example, because

Japanesc culture values face-saving, a Tokyo-based company would never reject an American offer with an outright *no*. However, saying, "we shall give it some consideration" is every bit as final. A high-context communicator is sensitive to situational data, i.e. implicit information. The priority is maintaining harmony. Communication is relationship- and feeling-focused as well as feminine in nature.

People in low-context cultures — Americans, Germans, Swiss — tend to be more direct. Things are explicit: clear, linear, verbal. Peter believes that words don't need to be interpreted when their content is evident: *no* means no, *yes* means yes and *horrible* means horrible. A low-context communicator is highly responsive to standardized data and explicit information. Communication is result-focused as well as masculine in nature.

In the business world, a low-context culture compartmentalizes personal relationships, work and the other aspects of day-to-day life. A German executive office is a closed room, a sort of hideaway for the boss which keeps distractions at a distance. Information communicated in the office is shared only with a select few. The result is a lack of extensive, well-developed information networks outside one's own special area of expertise. People need to receive detailed information before making a decision.

Low-context	**High-context**
Explicit	Implicit
Context not important	Context is everything
Thinking-focused	Feeling-focused
Result-oriented	Relationship-oriented
Masculine	Feminine

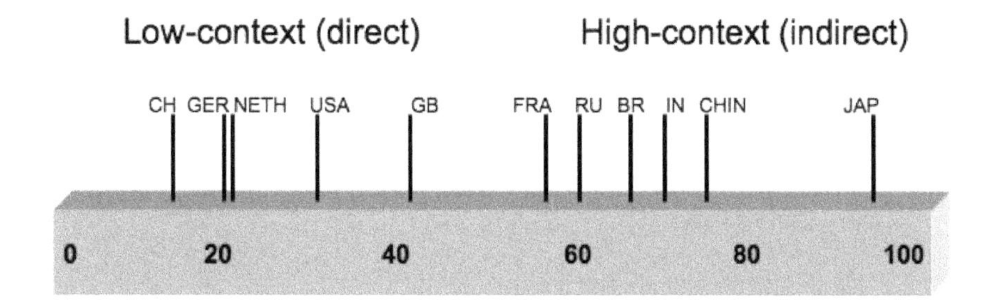

Case Study

CONFLICT BETWEEN HIGH- AND LOW-CONTEXT COMMUNICATION

Mixing high- and low-context communication can lead to confusion and may have severe consequences, as this example makes clear:

> A few years ago, an Air Florida jet crashed just after taking off from Washington, D.C. in icy conditions. Seventy four-people lost their lives. An investigation showed that the pilot had little experience of flying in icy weather. The co-pilot, who had more, had tried to dissuade him from taking off. The following was retrieved from the plane's "black box":
>
> > Co-pilot: "Do you see how the ice is hanging there at the back? Do you see it? Ice caps are all over."
> >
> > Pilot: "Hum, yeah."
> >
> > [The co-pilot expresses his worries about the long delay between de-icing and take-off.]
> >
> > Co-pilot: "De-icing is for all intents and purposes a hopeless battle, it gives you a false sense of security, that's all."
> >
> > [Just before take-off, the co-pilot mentions another problem: abnormal signals from the instrument panel. But, again, he doesn't insist on it once the pilot dismisses his concerns.]
> >
> > Co-pilot: "There is something not right here." [Three-second pause.] "This is not 0.K, really."
> >
> > Pilot: "Yes, it is. It's okay. It shows 80."
> >
> > Co-pilot: "Nah, I don't believe that's normal." [Seven-second pause.] "Oh, maybe it's okay..."
>
> Shortly after, the tragic accident occurred.

DIRECT AND INDIRECT COMMUNICATION

Put the following phrases in order from "'most direct" to 'most indirect'.
(You want somebody to pick up your clothes at the dry-cleaners.)

1.__ Could you possibly get my clothes?

2.__ Where do you think my clothes are?

3.__ Get my clothes.

4.__ I was wondering if you could pick up my clothes.

5.__ Would it bother you if I asked you to pick up my clothes?

6.__ Don't you think it's time we picked up my clothes?

7.__ Please pick up my clothes.

8.__ Have my clothes been picked up yet?

DIRECT AND INDIRECT COMMUNICATION

In the following sentences, write "D" if you think it's direct (low-context) and "I" if it's indirect (high-context).

1. __ "Let's get straight to the point!"

2. __ "Would it perhaps be possible to ask a question now?"

3. __ "You're fired as of this moment!"

4. __ "Gentlemen, let's stop beating around the bush. Who's at fault?"

5. __ "Your brand new Rolls Royce looks somewhat up-scale".

6. __ Chit-chatting before getting down to business.

7.__ Communication between an old married couple.

8. __ "You must read between the lines to understand the situation."

9. __ "If I may say so, I believe your analysis is somewhat unclear."

10.__"The situation must be bad because the captain has taken over the ship."

(Suggested answers on page 138)

"Deep cultural undercurrents structure life in subtle but highly consistent ways that are not consciously formulated. Like the invisible jet streams in the skies that determine the course of a storm, these currents shape our lives; yet their influence is only beginning to be identified."
— EDWARD HALL

Monochronic and Polychronic Behavior

Critical incident

What do you think is happening here?

> A Danish businessman, Stephan, is in Buenos Aires to meet his Argentinian counterpart for an important deal. Stephan has an appointment but, when he arrives at 10 a.m. sharp, he's told Luis is running late. Forty minutes later Luis shows up, gives Stephan a big hug and leads him into an office. But before they can get down to business, a secretary has documents for Luis to sign and then he has to take a call. By 11 o'clock, Stephan is wondering if his host is being disrespectful on purpose.

Commentary

Another important aspect of culture, according to Hall, is that of time. He points out that there are two approaches to time: monochronic and polychronic. In a monochronic society, time is seen as a valuable and finite resource. People concentrate on one given activity at a time. Time is linear and can be divided into segments and compartmentalized. Arriving punctually and keeping to a schedule are almost sacred.

Anglo-Saxon, Germanic and Scandinavian peoples are monochronic. Time is talked about as if it were a real, tangible object. Monochronic time is so ingrained in Stephean's thought-patterns that he feels it's nature-based. In fact, it's conditioned behavior which grew out of the Industrial Revolution in England. The factory required its labor force to be in place at scheduled times.

While a monochronic lifestyle appears to increase efficiency, it violates our biological rhythms. A more natural way of being is the polychronic system, the simultaneous occurrence of many activities which places more emphasis on people and relationships than on punctual performance. Latin and Arab cultures are polychronic. Two Italian businessmen are more likely to continue a conversation than to stop abruptly because of other appointments. Stephan is extremely unhappy about the course of events but he doesn't realize he and Luis live in two different time-systems.

The Japanese can be either monochronic and polychronic, depending on the situation. In a social context, they take time to nurture relationships but, in the workplace, are strictly monochronic.

Monochronic	**Polychronic**
One thing at a time	Multi-tasking
The job comes first	Work is subject to interruptions
Take deadlines seriously	Consider schedules as objectives to be met if possible
Are low-context and need information	Are high-context & already have knowledge
Are committed to results	Are committed to relationships
Adhere religiously to plans	Change directions often and easily
Concerned about not disturbing others, respect privacy	Intimacy between family, friends and close business associates
Respect for private property	Borrow and lend often and easily
Time is money	Relationships are most important

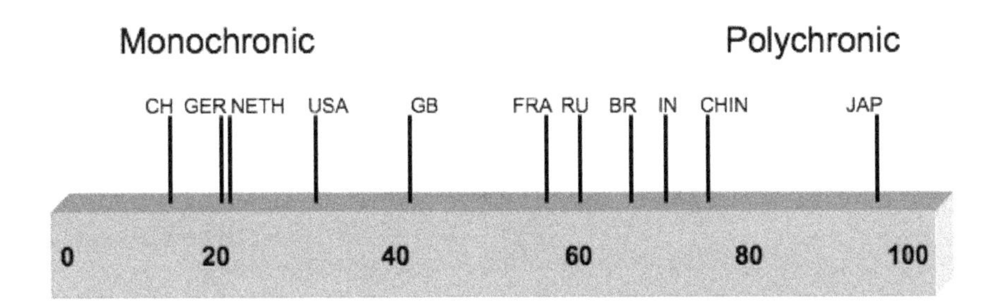

EXERCISE

MONOCHRONIC OR POLYCHRONIC

In the following sentences, mark "M" if you think the behavior is more likely monochronic, "P" if the contrary:

1. __ When I'm on the phone, please don't bother me.

2. __ Susan likes to do her homework while listening to the radio.

3. __ Brazilians always arrive half an hour late for a dinner invitation.

4. __If my father gets a call from a friend, he'll change his weekend plans at the last minute.

5. __ Manfred respects my privacy.

6. __ Bill Clinton spends endless hours with all kinds of people.

7. __ With Eric, you can be sure commitments will be honored.

8. __ Women seem less concerned about arriving on time than men.

9. __ The CEO is easily distracted and subject to continual interruptions by his secretaries.

10. __My cousin often talks on the phone while watching TV.

11. __Germans are famous for their punctuality.

12. __Mexicans don't seem too worried about being late.

13. __The deadline has to be respected.

14. __A good personnel director is committed to people.

15. __John felt insulted because he had to wait 40 minutes to see the manager.

(Suggested answers on page 138)

Case Study

Loss of Face in India

Nigel Turner, a British software engineer, has been sent to India to take over the supervision of a large team of Indian software developers. He's never been to India, but feels that his earlier experience in managing a multi-cultural team (American, Australian, Brazilian and French) will provide him with the necessary skills to get along with the Indians.

After a week on the job, he receives instructions from the London headquarters to immediately change the software development plan. He goes to Bharat, head of the development section, who is talking with his colleagues. Nigel tells Bharat to hold off on the coding of the specs of module 2 and start work immediately on module 3. Bharat says nothing, looks away rather uncomfortably. The other engineers, likewise, suddenly become quiet and appear troubled.

Noting the silence, Nigel tries to soften his demand: "Look Bharat, I know you don't want to change priorities, but the London office insists on it. Will there be a problem in carrying out the change?" Bharat doesn't look up and says, "Whatever you say, sir." Although the answer is evasive, at least in Nigel's mind, he has a commitment.

Three days later, when he checks to see how Bharat and his team are doing, Nigel finds that they're still working on module 2. When he asks him why, Bharat mumbles something and looks down.

What happened here?

Basically, Nigel committed a major faux pas in Indian society by telling Bharat to change plans in front of his subordinates. In the eyes of the other engineers, Bharat lost face because he appeared not to know more than the other engineers. As a manager, he is expected to have more information. Nigel should have made his request in a private setting.

Additionally, in India, an employee cannot question or contradict his boss. To do so would cause the senior person to lose face and the employee would be perceived as impolite and disrespectful.

Case Study

A "task-oriented" Dutchman in China

The Dutch production specialist Hans Schutz is being shown around the brand new production plant in Shanghai, which has just started to run. He's happy that his Chinese partners have received the state-of-the-art computers from the US, but is perplexed that they have not yet been installed. It would facilitate production immensely.

Six weeks later, he inspects the factory again and discovers that the computers still haven't been put into use. He asks his Chinese partner, Ching, what the problem is. Ching, somewhat embarrassed, explains that there are many electrical blackouts during the day. Hans can't believe the answer because if it were true, the rest of the plant wouldn't be operating. He asks himself why his Chinese counterpart can't tell him the truth to such a simple question.

What happened here?

This cross-cultural incident demonstrates the difference between being task-oriented and people-oriented cultures. Hans has been educated to concentrate on the task — the smooth functioning of the factory — and less on the personal relationships. Ching has been raised in an environment where "face" is the principal measure of an individual's reputation and dignity — both for himself and others.

For the Chinese, openingly admitting that they have no idea on how to install the computers would be a loss of "face". Although most Westerners understand this notion intellectually, they fail to really appreciate its importance in Asia. Additionally, Hans' communication style is likely to be too direct for high-context Chinese.

Case Study

Brazilian Commitment to Relationships at Work

Scott is an American accountant working in his company's subsidiary in Sao Paulo. He's been trying to finish an urgent cost-analysis report for headquarters, but can't because his subordinate, Carlos, still hasn't delivered the promised figures. Deciding he can't wait any longer, he goes to Carlos' office to see if a personal visit could speed things up.

As the American enters his office, the Brazilian colleague greets him warmly and starts asking about the weekend, his family and about how things are going in the office. Scott, after exchanging a few words about the family, gets down to business: "Look, I want to talk about the report I'm working on. I need those figures you promised last week." Carlos tells him in a friendly tone that the figures will be coming soon and continues talking again about the family. Scott can't believe his ears and reacts angrily: "Do you think I have all the time in the world? Knock off the small talk. Will I get the figures or not?" Seeing his displeasure, Carlos picks up the phone and calls a colleague. The American mutters to himself, "He still hasn't got the figures! Typical Brazilian."

On the phone, Carlos talks to his colleague about the weather, the family, the football game and then says: "José, I have a small problem. My American boss is in my office and wants to have those figures I told you about. Can you e-mail them to him?" As he puts the phone down, he tells Scott, "Those figures will be e-mailed to you in five minutes." The American leaves the office muttering, "And I had to waste my time talking about the family just to get those figures."

What happened here?

This is a conflict between linear thinking that favors practicality and efficiency and that of circular logic that emphasizes intimacy between family, friends and close business associates. Carlos found his American colleague to be very aggressive, too direct and above all unfriendly. Good relations and being interested in others is important for any business. Scott thought Carlos didn't take his job seriously, let alone deadlines. What's more, the Brazilian didn't know how to communicate in a straight and factual manner. All this talk about everything except business suggested to Scott that Carlos was trying to hide something.

To reduce such misunderstandings, both sides need to understand and empathize with the situation in which others work. This is best done through an intercultural training course.

Business Suggestions For Working In

Collectivist cultures

- Be patient, things take time
- Work within the group
- Don't expect immediate feedback
- Allow people to discuss new information
- Get support of key members (integrate)
- Avoid singling out individuals
- Praise the group
- Do not push for decisions on the spot

Individualist cultures

- Accept individual responsibilities
- Give praise for top performance
- Stimulate individual initiative within the team
- Promote yourself
- Act quickly following an agreement
- Don't rely on others
- Recognize individual contributions
- Make decisions quickly

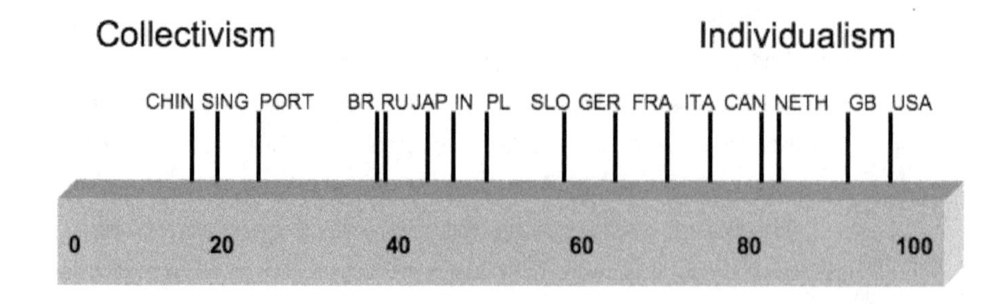

Business Suggestions
For Working In

Low-hierarchy cultures

- Allow information to flow at all levels
- Consult your subordinates
- Keep people informed of company goals
- Do not expect respect just because of your reputation or position
- Demonstrate competence, not seniority
- Learn to delegate
- Show initiative / be assertive

High-hierarchy cultures

- Allow information to flow top-down
- Instruct subordinates what to do
- Outline procedures clearly
- Allow time to build relationships
- Expect reluctance when people have to make decisions
- Enforce project deadlines strictly
- Recognize hierarchy (and seniority) in meetings, negotiations and company parties
- Moderate personal initiative as it may be seen as immodest

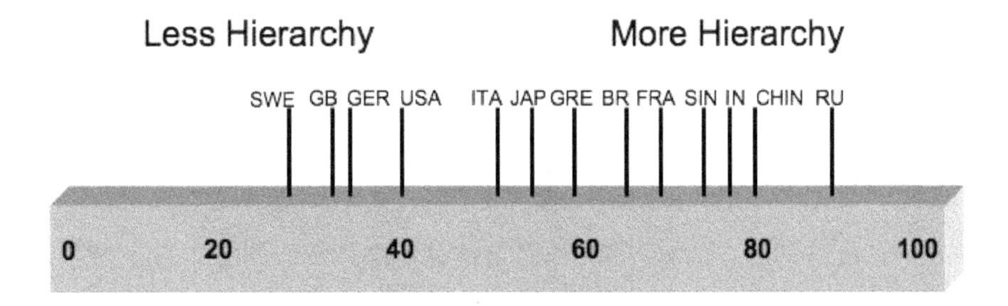

Business Suggestions For Working In

Low-structure cultures

- Ask questions when unsure
- Learn to work with as few rules as possible
- Don't be afraid of making mistakes
- Take risks — failure is an opportunity to learn
- Be pragmatic and make short-term plans
- Be tolerant of ambiguity
- Don't take criticism personally, it's part of the job and goes no further

High-structure cultures

- Reassure people around you more often
- Allow more time for planning
- Announce changes ahead of time and implement them as quickly as possible
- Dedicate more time to solving conflicts
- Be responsive to people's problems
- Promote harmony, not competition, within a team
- Demonstrate polite persistence as it will be rewarded in the long run

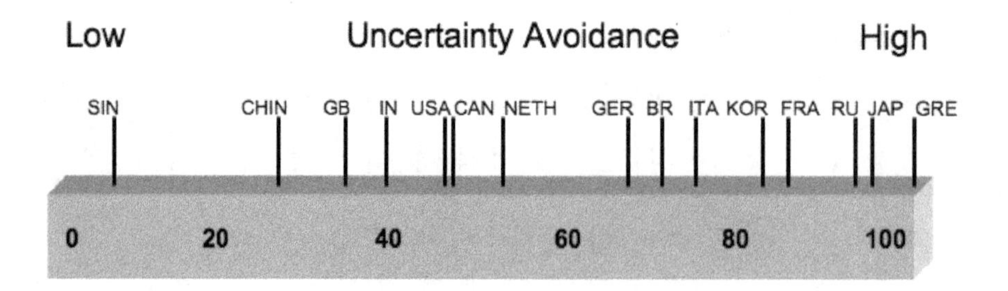

Business Suggestions
For Working In

Feminine cultures

- Take the time to know and cooperate with colleagues
- Develop a sense of solidarity; friendliness is more important than brilliance
- Don't overtly display achievement
- Learn to tolerate an open display of emotions
- Appreciate expressions of goodwill regardless of significance to business
- Remember consensus and harmony are social cornerstones

Masculine cultures

- Recognize that business comes first
- Caring for others comes second or not at all
- Recognize individual achievement and praise success
- Learn to promote yourself unflinchingly
- Displaying material success is viewed as positive
- Showing solidarity doesn't have as much relevance as performance

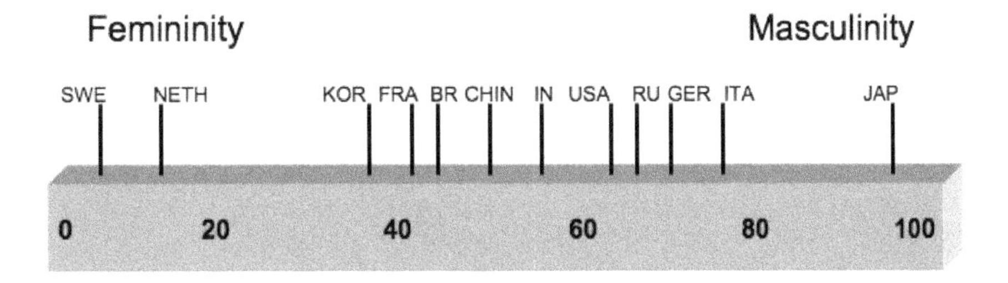

Business Suggestions For Working In

Low-context cultures

- Always be concise
- Answer e-mails, faxes and letters promptly; return phone calls
- Concentrate on the literal meaning of words
- Structure meetings with an agenda
- Don't be offended by confrontations
- Begin reports with a concise summary
- Deal with facts (control your feelings)
- Understand that dissent (even strong) is seldom personal

High-context cultures

- Avoid direct *yes* or *no* questions
- Use qualifiers such as "maybe", "possibly", etc.
- Ask for written confirmation of directions
- Avoid putting people on the spot
- Don't be impatient
- Remain open to alternative solutions
- Consider an employee's entire situation before passing judgment
- Expect personal issues to interfere with performance

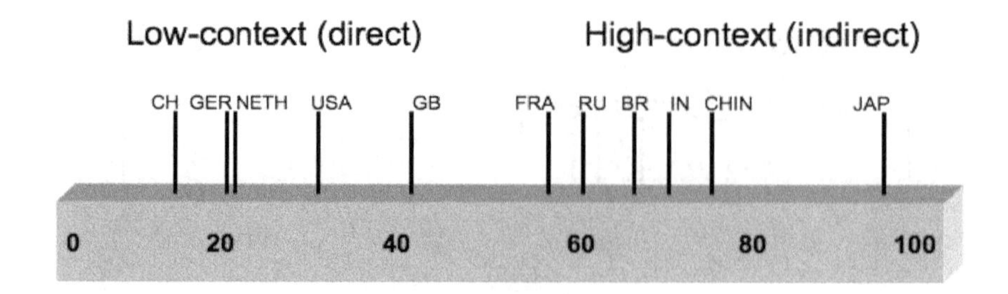

Business Suggestions For Working In

Monochronic cultures

- Report delays without delay!
- Be as detailed and specific as possible
- Plan ahead (even though you expect plans to be changed)
- Keep strictly to appointments
- Focus on one activity at a time (management-by-objectives)

Polychronic cultures

- Set "realistic" deadlines (checkpoints)
- Build in extra time (artificial deadlines)
- Keep in close contact with colleagues / subordinates (ask for status reports)
- Give relationships precedence over schedules
- Accept interruptions and (apparent) lack of focus
- Learn to appreciate the history and traditions of a company
- Confirm meetings and other business engagements

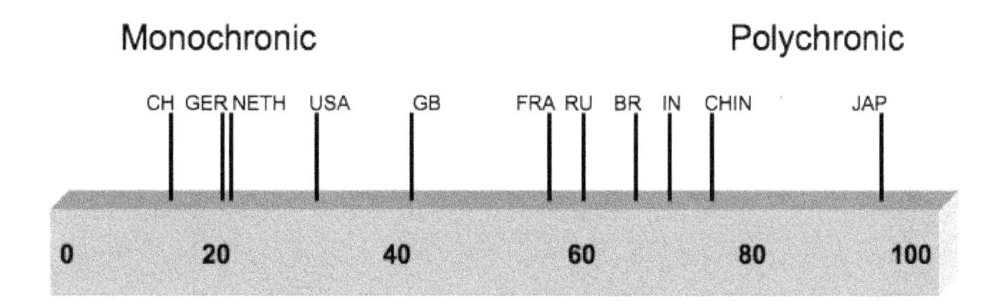

II

Comm

Communication

Defining Communication

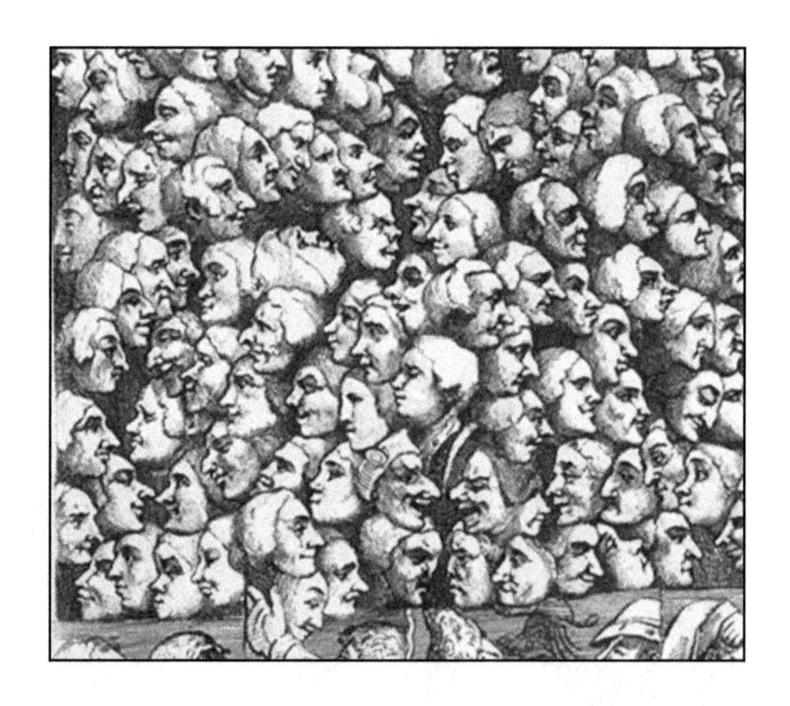

Take a look at the following breakdown in communication between an American and a Chinese:

> Frank from San Francisco has been negotiating intensively on an important deal for two weeks in Shanghai. He finally comes to an agreement with Chang. To celebrate, his Chinese counterpart invites the American for dinner in an exclusive restaurant that evening. Not to be outdone, Frank looks for a suitable gift. In an antique shop he finds a beautiful double clock — the ideal present to indicate time both in Shanghai and San Francisco. He goes back to his hotel room and wraps it with white paper. Seeing the present, Chang doesn't want to accept it. Frank, however, insists that he open it. When he discovers the clocks, the Chinese businessman turns white. Chang tells Frank that not only is the dinner off, but the deal as well.
>
> Why did Chang have a sudden change of heart? The Chinese are superstitious due to their cultural upbringing. White is worn at funerals to express sorrow and the word "clock" has the same sound as "death". By offering a clock wrapped in white, Frank was bringing, in Chang's eyes, an untimely symbolic message.

This is a classic case of American value for time clashing with Chinese superstitious beliefs. The source of cultural misunderstandings is due to the age-old human tendency to interpret "foreign" behavior in terms of our own cultural experience. Frank projects his cultural values on to Chang and is surprised when his Chinese counterpart seems uncomfortable and angry.

To overcome these misunderstandings, we first need to define the term communication. "It's the process by which individuals try to exchange ideas, feelings, symbols, meanings to create commonality.". Communication includes both sending verbal messages (words) and non-verbal messages (pauses, attitude, tone of voice, voice, physical appearance, etc). It is a *symbolic process* in which people create shared meanings.

In communication, messages aren't directly received, but rather indirectly. It begins with the sender, who has a thought. It is transformed into a symbolical format, such as sounds (spoken language), body language, e-mail, fax and sent to the receiver. This is known as *encoding*. The meanings of the symbols are then translated by the receiver by a process of *decoding* (see figure below).

When the sender and the receiver have the same background, communication usually works smoothly. The danger of any *decoding*, however, lies when the receiver comes from another culture with different rules and values. This is intercultural communication — the process by which people create symbolic meanings, based on their own assumptions and beliefs, which they send to others who do not inherently share the same values.

Another way to understand this American-Chinese misunderstanding is to imagine that your mind functions like an automatic pilot. When you're in your home environment, almost all of your movements and thoughts occur subconsciously, intuitively. The moment you're outside of that environment, the automatic pilot has problems finding its bearings. The intelligent decision is to take over the plane's controls yourself and observe the foreign culture.

This is easier said than done. When we meet someone in a foreign setting and discover that he or she can speak our language, we often unconsciously fall back

The Communication Process

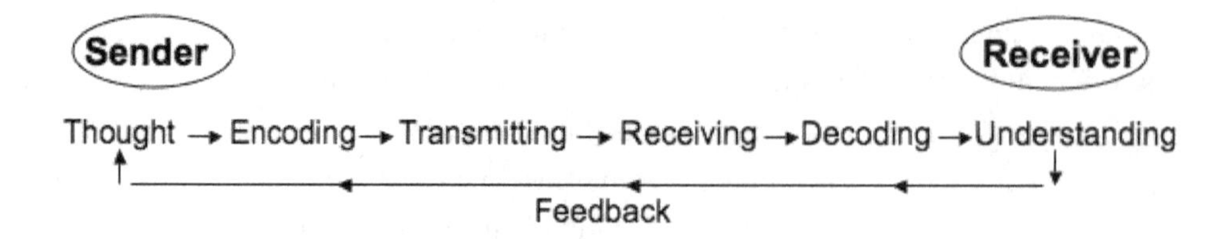

into our normal mode. There's nothing wrong with that as long as the agenda is non-controversial, such as asking for directions.

Real problems begin when we touch on unspoken reflexes, hidden assumptions — even something as seemingly simple as notions like "clock" and "white". Our cultural identity prompts us to have negative feelings toward anybody who doesn't share our values. At this point, the communication process starts breaking down, leaving us with a sense of frustration and confusion. Our instinctive response is ethnocentrism — to categorize people into two classes: "we" and "they". "We" is my tribe, which my group says is rational, good, and reasonable, whereas "they", that tribe over there, are mysterious, strange and potentially dangerous.

Instead of realizing that misunderstandings are caused by *communication styles with different rules and norms*, people tend to think the problem is *the other person's character.*

Confucius once said: "By nature men are all alike — by practice they have become far apart." The human heart is the same all over the world but our habits, expectations and behavior are shaped by cultural conditioning. And even if it were possible to send a message without any cultural influences, the receiver will automatically interpret it through the filter of their own cultural conditioning. That alone makes the communication process much more difficult and challenging than we think.

"People put a great deal of time and effort into becoming well-socialized members of their own culture. They develop a view of the world that makes sense to them. When they discover people of other cultures have a different view, some of their fundamental assumptions about life are challenged."

– Richard Brislin

A "Mirror Finish"
A Misunderstanding in Communication

Boeing contracted a Japanese supplier to produce fuselage panels for its 767 aircraft, stipulating in the contract that the panels should have a "mirror finish". The costs for the part were considerably higher than expected because the supplier thought that the panels had to be polished and polished to have a literally "mirror-like" exterior. Imagine the surprise of the Japanese when they found out that all Boeing wanted was a clean, shiny surface.

Linguistic Blunders in English

The following examples depict the difficulties non-native English speakers have when trying to speak or write. Although they may have spent several years studying the language, they still make many syntactical and grammatical mistakes. Our mind is essentially conditioned by habits, which hinders our ability to imitate and master the linguistic patterns of another language.

In a Bucharest hotel lobby: "The lift is being fixed for the next day. During that time we regret that you will be unbearable."

A shopping bag in Zurich showing yachts on a blue lake with the caption: "Switzerland: Seaside City."

A German ordering a hamburger in New York: "Waiter, I'd like to become a hamburger."

Warning to motorists in Tokyo: "When a passenger of the foot heave in sight, tootle the horn. Trumpet at him melodiously at first, but if he still obstacles your passage, then tootle him with vigor."

On a menu of a Swiss restaurant: "Our wines leave you nothing to hope for."

At a Hong Kong dentist: "Teeth extracted by the latest Methodists."

At a Greek tailors: "Order your summer suit. Because a big rush we will execute customers in strict rotation."

In a Copenhagen airline office: "We take your bags and send them in all directions."

Instructions on a packet of food from Italy: "Besmear a backing pan, previously buttered with a good tomato sauce, and, after, dispose the cannelloni, lightly distanced between them in a only couch."

On every door in a hotel in Sarajevo, Bosnia: "Guests should announce the abandonment of their rooms before 12 o'clock."

When learning a foreign language is so laborious, just imagine how hard it is to understand and identify with other people's values and assumptions.

"The Tower of Babel", *by the Dutch 16th century painter Pieter Bruegel, refers to the story in the biblical Book of Genesis. In it, the people of the world are all united and speak a common language. They begin to build a tower to reach the heavens and become godlike themselves. God, seeing this, decides to prevent this by confusing the language of the people and destroying the tower. When the people can no longer understand each other, they give up work on the tower and spread out to different parts of the world. This portrayal of humanity ultimately explores the notion that we are all intimately connected on a birth-and-death level, yet the subtle differences of language and the frustrating inability to communicate breaks us apart. In our current globalized world of instant communication and faster and cheaper transportation, the destroyed Babel tower becomes even more relevant.*

In 2006, film director Alejandro Gonzalez Inarritu takes this metaphor and uses it as the title of his Academy-Award winning film "Babel". *As the legend implies, it's about the difficulty of human communication. Although the stories are set in several countries and in five languages— English, Arabic, Spanish, Japanese and sign, language is far from being the main barrier. Instead, the film looks at the ways in which cultural assumptions and biases tend to hide reality even when reality is clear, and the manner in which our perceived differences prevent us from relating to one another as human beings.. It's original cinema, one that is thought-provoking, emotional and brilliant.*

THREE APPROACHES TO INTERCULTURAL COMMUNICATION

Before discussing barriers to intercultural communication, it would be useful at this point to see how different theoretical orientations provide an overall understanding of cross-cultural interactions. The three approaches below are derived from the lectures given by Dr. Milton Bennett at Winterthur, Switzerland in May 2006; the examples given, however, are from the author.

Positivist (Comparative anthropology): Classic anthropology is defined as the comparative study of human societies and their development. Studying cultural artifacts (art, architecture, music, literature) and the social, economic and political systems provides you with an overall general understanding of a country. In other words, the focus is on what can be empirically measured or tangibly perceived. For example, social scientists might closely observe the Japanese rituals of greeting and its historical development. Or investigate the historical reasons why the British prefer "fish and chips" as their national food. Additionally, a list of *do's and don'ts* provides rules for proper behavior. Although cultural knowledge is in itself interesting and useful for a short briefing of a country, its static nature isn't able to interface with the dialectic nature of intercultural encounters.

Relativist (Cross-cultural psychology): In this model, cultural differences are described in terms of value-orientations within a system. The most influential theoretical models are those of Geert Hofstede and Edward T. Hall. Beliefs and patterns, such as individualism and collectivism or communication style, are observed within systems. By contrasting countries, you reduce value projections, allowing for more cultural awareness and an understanding of the relativity of values. For instance, Americans are distinguished from the Germans by a much higher level of risk taking. However, this doesn't lead to real intercultural communication as adaptation occurs only through role enactment and the subconscious assumption of similarities (sympathy). Essentially, one doesn't move out of one's cultural boundaries.

Constructivist (Cognitive psychology): The constructivist approach explains at best how real intercultural communication emerges. It draws its inspiration and concepts from cognitive psychology rather than personality psychology. Instead of assuming similarity, it assumes that there are differences in the knowledge structure, the "mental software" that decides people's thoughts and actions. To understand and communicate with other cultures, both parties must be prepared to penetrate dynamically into the other person's mind (empathy). Like a good actor who can identify with his or her character, you enact how the other feels. For example, John F. Kennedy's famous sentence "*Ich bin ein Berliner*" in front of the Berlin Wall in 1963 made him the idol of the Germans. Kennedy felt and internalized the perspective of the Berliners and then enacted it through role behavior. All influential and historical figures as well as successful expatriates possess this empathic skill. This interconnecting model is the one most likely to lead to "cultural adaptation".

John Kennedy's famous words "Ich bin ein Berliner" not only sent a powerful message towards his German listeners, but demonstrated also his empathy for their concerns.

Three Applications of Intercultural Communication

Derived from Milton J. Bennett

	Positivist	Relativist	Constructivist
Assumption	Reality is absolute and discoverable	Reality is framed by an observer's perspective, formed within "systems".	Reality emerges from transaction between observer and observed.
Implication	Discover what is real and unreal in a culture. Assumes 'finished' artifacts, non-movement.	Culture is a set of roles and rules within a social system. Awareness of other perspective	Culture is socially constructed. Conscious of own boundary-setting.
Application	Adaptation is knowledge of cultural history. Enactment of "do's & don't's"	Learn about cultures through contrast analysis. "Informed" role play (sympathy)	Adaptation is dynamic, 'other' perspective-taking (empathy). Mutual penetration

Communication Contrast:

AMERICAN, GERMAN AND CHINESE

Another approach in overcoming intercultural misunderstandings is to examine communication styles. When describing the interaction style of others, we are actually referring to the *psychology of a people*, i.e. their mental and emotional processes. This leads to an interesting question: why have groups chosen different values and norms, resulting in different communication modes? The answer can be found by going into that innate part of thought, known as "basic assumptions".

The Americans

American communication is relatively low-context, what is said is what is meant. Americans get straight to the point and want to know the intentions of others. Yet, at the same time, they want to *be liked*. This explains why they are more direct than Germans or Swiss, when it comes to expressing pleasure, giving compliments or revealing personal details to people they don't know well.

Eagerness to get results

The one characteristic that sets Americans apart from other nationalities is their obsession with getting results, i.e. making money fast. "Time is money", "let's wheel and deal", "we don't care what you do or how you do it as long as it gets done", "time-management" and "what's the bottom line?" are all popular expressions.

The famous Mount Rushmore majestically depicts four Presidents — George Washington, Thomas Jefferson, Theodore Roosevelt and Abraham Lincoln — symbolizing the American free spirit.

Americans want to get

down to business as quickly as possible. They have little inclination to get to know the other person. A typical attitude is "Why fool around chit-chatting when we could be making deals?" This reflects itself in tightly-framed meetings with set time-limits, designed to obtain rapid agreements. Generally, Americans don't want to think in complex terms or discuss hypothetical situations, as it holds up the pace.

Because they're perpetually in a hurry, they squeeze every minute they can into their working day.

"The American dream is often a very private dream of being the star, the uniquely successful and admirable one, the one who stands out from the crowd of ordinary folk who don't know how."
— from the collection
HABITS OF THE HEART (1986)

Inductive Thinking

American thought processes are trained to be inductive: first making empirical observations, then collecting and analyzing data, to finally deriving principles. This pattern of thought has been characterized as procedural thinking, in which a sequence of individual points are focused on and solved before moving on to the bigger picture.

Perceived as being restless, Americans like to claim that "progress" has been made once a few points have been agreed upon. This can be quite confusing for Europeans, who are generally deductive by nature. They don't think it makes any sense to discuss the individual points until there is a "mutual understanding" of the complete situation.

Informality

Parallel to getting straight to the point is the generally informal atmosphere that prevails. Americans like informality because it speeds things up and makes the participants feel at ease. A formal manner may be interpreted as being aloof or pretentious. This explains, in part, why Americans are good at forming quick, if disposable, relationships. Typically, you'll hear "Let's not waste time on formalities. My name's Bob. What's yours?"

The American desire for "egalitarianism" is also at work here. Historically, there has been relatively little importance attached to titles. Nothing will make an American angrier than arbitrary ranking by class. American managers will go out of their way to display camaraderie with their subordinates. In an effort to appear "one of the gang" the manager might put his feet on his desk and invite everyone to call him by his first name. Despite this display, everyone is well aware who is in command.

Simplicity

Americans are time-conscious ("time is money") and their speech and writing patterns are generally concise. Communication is based on pragmatic thinking, like newspaper headlines — short and to the point. A line of thought is conceived in terms of efficiency: the shortest distance between two points is a straight line. All this starts at school, where students are taught that simplicity is the key to good writing.

Not much time is spent on developing complicated, philosophical ideas, as it is thought to be inefficient. Americans want the essential information. Although this can be regarded by foreigners as superficiality, a pragmatic communication style has its positive side. Americans are very good at rapid-fire, improvisational speaking. In meetings, they are able to toss wild and often playful ideas around. Commonly known as brainstorming, it comes as second-nature to most Americans, part of "thinking on one's feet". It is also one of the reasons for the American talent for innovation.

Most Americans are not subtle in their conversations. Thoughts aren't generally carried to the second, let alone the third level. For this reason they may feel uncomfortable with refined, indirect statements and often miss nonverbal cues, such as a slight shift in tone or a subtle change in body posture or breathing. When a European is trying to discreetly get the message across that something is wrong, an American may not catch on. And missed hints can cause situations to explode.

Exaggeration and humor

Matching their infinite optimism and constant need to sell themselves, Americans love to overstate things. Their enthusiasm, for example, can reach levels of absurdity for a non-American (It's *fantastic* to see you again. *Wow*, you look *great!*)

They like to use humor in their conversations. To have a good sense of humor is a must if someone wants to get ahead. An effective speech usually begins with an anecdote or a joke. At a social gathering or party, Americans tend to avoid serious or intellectual discussions and prefer a light form of small talk: chit-chatting.

The Germans

German communication places strong emphasis on content and downplays personal relationships in order to be *credible* and *objective*. Germans belong to a low-context culture and expect data-oriented, detailed information and instruction to guide them in the performance of their task.

Johann Wolfgang von Goethe is considered to be the Shakespeare of German literature. His works not only heavily influenced German thinking, but were also a primary source of inspiration in music, drama, poetry, and philosophy across Europe.

Importance of Extensive Background Information

Before any agreement is reached, Germans want to be sure they have all the relevant facts. They tend to look to historical precedents to understand the present. Thus, an introductory speech will include a lot of background information, giving a breadth of perspective that many Americans would leave out.

The German style is to fill each part of an explanation with details to avoid uncertainty and ambiguity. Presentations can be long, but Germans are conditioned to this and are patient listeners. The tendency to be excessively analytical and complex may be perceived by other nationalities as over-doing it, a sort of "paralysis through analysis".

Like Americans, Germans expect visuals and lots of figures to illustrate the points being made. The difference is that they tend to provide more information than most Americans think they need.

Confrontational and direct

The main objective in a German conversation is to get at the truth of an issue. Germans value frankness and are not afraid to explore all sides of a topic, even if it means being unpleasant and hurting other people's feelings. They are generally more direct than Americans, especially when it comes to stating facts, offering criticism and giving commands. Foreigners often find this style overly-aggressive and even impolite.

> "In action, the English have the advantage enjoyed by free men always entitled to free discussion: of having a ready judgment on every question. We Germans, on the other hand, are always thinking. We think so much that we never form a judgment."
>
> — Heinrich Heine

Additionally, German words have a hard, guttural sound with sharp, yet monotone speech patterns. It's a language that sounds as if it gets things done. For a non-German, though, it may come across as rough and even "domineering".

Formalism

The Germans perceive themselves as being polite and expect visitors to behave accordingly. The American manner of getting to know their counterparts by saying "just call me Joe" is not naturally accepted by Germans who have a strong sense of privacy. What it comes down to is that Germans feel uncomfortable with what they perceive as "promiscuous familiarity".

Protocol dictates that the first thing to do at a meeting is to shake hands with everyone. As Germans respect hierarchy, the highest-ranking visitor is expected to introduce himself or herself. The other members of the team introduce themselves by seniority. Each person gives a brief description of their area of responsibility. Then the hosts introduce themselves in turn.

During a break, Germans don't normally "shoot the breeze" (an expression which has no equivalent in the German language). Life is seen as too serious to waste time on nonsense. When non-business subjects are discussed, even trivial matters like sports or vacation plans, it is done in depth and in an earnest tone.

Understated Salesmanship

Germans are determined to make sure that they do things correctly and only want solid information. Wild Hollywood-like gesticulation and hard-sell talk won't go down well. Besides, jokes and humor are considered to be unhelpful distractions. Cartoon-style images on charts and graphs don't mix with business in the German mind. Likewise, attacking your competitors' products is not the way Germans operate. In their minds, a product or idea that is good will stand on its own merits. There's no need to put down the competitor.

A Wariness of Immediate Results

Germans are not obsessed with quick results. Although it may exasperate Americans, their strategy is, as previously mentioned, to think in the long term without worrying too much about immediate returns. Their habit of carefully weighing alternatives makes them, as one astute observer noted, "systematically pragmatic".

Case Study

American Optimism or German Realism?

Günter Rommel works for a large publishing company in Stuttgart. One year ago, his firm put out a book with an American publisher in Los Angeles, a venture which turned out to be highly successful. There had, however, been a few glitches. He was then sent to Southern California to discuss a new venture and to make sure that the problems did not occur again.

During his stay, Günter found the weather to be wonderful and sunny, like his American counterparts. They literally behaved like "sonny boys". Every time he attempted to discuss potential conflicts and problems, his partners told him, in excessively exuberant voices, not to worry; there were no problems, only "challenges". Günter perceived their continually rosy outlook as superficial and complained that they were not being honest with him. The Americans answered that he was too pessimistic, making mountains out of molehills. During lunch, an American colleague, who Günter got along well with, took him aside and advised him to stop complaining, pointing out it would get him marked as a "loser" in the U.S.

Afterwards, back in his hotel room, Günter felt confused. Here he was, trying to do his job properly and when he gave honest criticism, he was branded as a complainer. He felt Americans always wanted to put a positive spin on things and gave the impression they didn't have their feet on the ground. Günter concluded that Americans didn't really have a grasp of reality and were shallow.

Was Günter correct in his assessment of the American character?

What happened here?

There are distinct differences between German and American communication styles, which often cause significant misunderstandings. As explained on the preceding pages, German conversation places strong emphasis on content and downplays personal relationships in order to appear *credible* and *objective*. Americans, on the other hand, accentuate both the content and personal in order to be *liked* and *socially accepted*.

There are also differing approaches to solving problems. The German tendency to analyze a situation in depth before taking any action is seen negatively by the Americans, who feel that it prevents things from getting done ("paralysis through analysis".) The US attitude is to try out ideas and see if they work ("trial and error").

The Chinese

Chinese communication, unlike American and German, is high-context. It is indirect, ambiguous and circular. The emphasis is on *developing relationships* and not on information gathering. Often the real meaning, especially if it is negative, is implied. As it is context-centered, the emphasis is not so much on what is said, but more on how it is said, who said it and what is behind what is said. What is left unsaid can be just as important, or more important than what has been said.

Need for harmony

In stark contrast to the German need for truth (and to a certain extent American as well), the Chinese consider the search for harmony and virtue far more important. This is tightly interwoven in the three fundamental aspects of Chinese culture: harmony, face and relationships. These three principles are derived from the ancient book *I Ching*, considered to be the base of Chinese thought.

Confucius and Lao-Tse, China's most revered philosophers, whose teachings have deeply influenced Chinese, Japanese, Korean and Vietnamese thought and life.

The work is based on the Taoist philosophy, where *Qi* (pronounced "chee") is seen as a universal energy. The need to be in harmony with *Qi* is attained through the interplay of two polarities —*yin* and *yang*.

Confucius later used this principle for his writings on harmony and balance in all aspects of life: the relationship networks at work *(guanxi)* and in the family, incorporating seniority and hierarchy.

Saving Face

One of the main tenets of Confucianism is face, the mark of personal dignity. The Chinese will go to great lengths to save face for themselves and their interlocutors. To avoid saying "no", the Chinese may use silence, implying "There are still problems, and we would like to reconsider the main issues".

Another way to avoid a negative response is to say *yanjiu yanjiu*, "we will do some research and discuss it later." The word "research" shouldn't be taken literally, for in many cases, it means "We're not interested". If there's a problem, they might avoid it all together. If a mistake has been made, it should never be communicated directly. Instead, it's often communicated indirectly, in the form of a tale with a moral.

Long-term Relationships

Many Westerners, especially Americans, conduct business in a no-nonsense "let's get right down to business" manner. Chinese interpret this as a sign of bad upbringing and even lack of morals. In China, all business begins with developing a relationship. The process is more important than the goal itself. Thus, meals are seen as an important ingredient in relationship building, a social lubricant rather than a waste of time. Good business means knowing your counterpart well. Once trust has been established, you may enter into the network of *guanxi*, a system where people are interrelated and expected to help each other at some point in time. This kind of interconnecting relationship contributes to a constructive cycle of harmony and reciprocity.

Unequal Relationships

There is high-power distance in Chinese culture. Harmony and stability are based on the Confucian idea of unequal relationships — the ruler and his subjects, the father and his sons, husband and wife, employer and employee. In corporate life, Chinese subordinates expect their superiors to tell them what to do. Failure to observe these rules would, in Chinese thinking, lead to anarchy, disorder and crime. While authority must not be questioned, those at the top must also fulfill their responsibility to protect and lead.

"A single conversation with a wise man is better than ten years of study."
— Chinese Proverb

In Chinese groups, there's usually an appointed leader who controls the discussion and the other members are expected to agree. Leaders will express opinions clearly and at times can be assertive. Whereas conversation of Americans could be described as "discussion", the Chinese way is close to "public speech".

As opposed to the Japanese style of prudence, Chinese are in comparison less hesitant to express disagreement, in a polite but obvious manner.

A "Non-Revealing" Body Language

The facial language of a Chinese is one of respect and reserve. They'll typically display a politely "blank" face during introductions. It reflects the Confucian idea that concealing emotions is a virtue. A spirit of modesty and humility prevails and politeness is observed. Their pace will be slow and repetitious, negotiating step by step in an unhurried manner.

Chinese Proverbs

Proverbs and idioms say much about people's traditional ways of experiencing reality, about values and warnings, and rules and wisdom which the elders want to impress on the minds of their young. The following are taken from Sun Tzu's Taoist-based "thirty-six strategies", dating back about 1,500 years. They are very much a part of China's overall heritage and provide us with remarkable insights into Chinese thinking.

"Walk the sheep home, just because it is there."

What the Chinese mean is "Take the opportunity to pilfer a goat." While carrying out your plans, be flexible enough to take advantage of any opportunity that presents itself, however small, and avail yourself of any profit, however slight.

"Scare the snake by hitting the grass."

When you cannot detect the opponent's plans, launch an unexpected but brief attack and observe your opponent's reactions. His behavior will reveal his strategy.

"If all else fails, retreat."

This is the most famous one of the 36th strategies: run away to fight another day. If it becomes obvious that your current course of action will lead to defeat, then retreat and regroup. When your side is losing, there are only three choices remaining: surrender, compromise, or escape. Surrender is complete defeat, compromise is half defeat, but escape is not defeat. As long as you are not defeated, you still have a chance.

Universal Non-Verbal Communication

The influence of non-verbal codes in language has been well documented. In fact, back in 1872 Charles Darwin noted the importance of these "hidden signals" and believed that certain non-verbal actions were universal, free from cultural influence. Research on facial expressions indicates the universality of many non-verbal emotional displays, confirming Darwin's hypothesis. For example take the emotion of fear, demonstrated by wide-open eyes, raised eyebrows, partially open mouth. Because this reaction appears to be consistent across cultures, there is probably a biological or genetic basis that permits this to appear in all humans.

Communication is not only using verbal codes. Equally important is non-verbal behavior, such as eye contact and touch, that may be biologically or genetically based. The 18th century painter James Barry depicts this splendidly in his well known work "Jupitor beguiled by Juno".

Barriers to Intercultural Communication

Language.

Critical incident

What do you think is happening here?

> A German executive, fluent in English, reads Bill Clinton's autobiography *My Life*. To his great surprise, he finds that on almost every third or fourth page, Bill Clinton writes about this or that "good friend". By the end of the book, he figures that the former President must have over 200 "good friends". How was that possible, he asks? In German culture, a person has at most two or three "good friends".

As mentioned in the chapter on socialization, language exerts an enormous power over the mind's ability to perceive and react to experience. In the above example, there is a clash of understanding between the German and American concept of "friend". For Germans friendship is a serious matter. It tends to be highly selective, profound and entails long-term commitment as well as depth of (unspoken) feeling.

The notion of friendship is not defined so clearly in the US. Many visitors make the mistake of equating American friendliness with friendship. What foreigners fail to understand is that Americans are guided by values of egalitarianism. At the outset, nobody is considered better or worse than anybody else. Therefore, the need for commitment is not strong and the message sent is rather: "I am friendly and approachable."

> "The limits of my language are the limits of my world."
>
> – Ludwig Wittgenstein

What we can learn from the above incident is that language is not only a tool for communication, but additionally it is a system of organizing perception and thinking. It affects how we experience and understand reality, which in turn "encourages habitual patterns of perception". To understand the effects of language on intercultural communications, consider the following question:

> *Does a person who learns to speak and write English, when growing up in Arkansas, "see" and "experience" the world differently than a person who learns to speak and write German in Hamburg?*

According to anthropologist Edward Sapir, the answer is yes. He articulated his theory of linguistic relativity in 1921: *We see and hear and otherwise experience very largely as we do because the language habits of our community predispose certain choices of interpretation*. Sapir's student, Benjamin Whorf went further and wrote: *Language plays a powerful role in determining the way in which we understand our reality*. Sapir/ Whorf theories provide an explanation on how Bill Clinton's interpretation of "good friend" is a learned language routine that is quite different from that of the German executive.

There are other examples of language habits to be found. A Texan in semi-tropical Houston looks at snow differently than an Inuit (Eskimo) in snow-covered Alaska. Whereas a Texan has only a few words for "snow", an Inuit has a large number (up to 20) for the same concept . This confirms Sapir's theory that language habits in our cultural environment sway us to certain interpretations.

"If the Romans had been obliged to learn Latin, they would never have found time to conquer the world."
—Heinrich Heine

Not only does language shape our outlook on the world, it can also indicate social status within a society. For instance, many languages, including German, French and Spanish, have informal and formal forms of the personal pronoun "you"; its application depends on the relationship between the speaker and the person addressed.

Or take the English verb *to know*. In Spanish, French and German, there are two meanings: one is used to characterize knowledge through experience and the other to articulate memorized information. To know Shanghai through experience is not the same as to know the exact words of Hamlet in Shakespeare's famous play.

Effective intercultural competence requires a dynamic consciousness of how our own language influences our interpretation of reality. Our mother tongue predisposes us to make certain distinctions and not others. It alone can act as a powerful mental block in hindering our ability to change our attitudes or adopt new approaches. In view of the interlocking nature of our own language and thought, cultural misunderstandings can be seen as a "clash of differing realities".

The Interlocking Nature of Language and Thought

Benjamin Whorf developed the theory that language plays a powerful role in conditioning our way of thinking and perception of reality. What he meant was, we act and live in a certain manner because our mental patterns are mostly shaped and embedded by the language we speak. In essence, our learned vocabulary reflects what is critical to survival and adaptation. For instance, people in the United States tend to act and live quickly because their mental thoughts are formulated along the American standard "time is money" which is considerably different from, let's say, the French "savoir vivre", which places importance on proper behavior.

The following text deals with the notion of rejection, written by a Chinese-English journalist. Remember that in Asian cultures, saving face is an extremely important value.

CHINESE EDITOR'S REJECTION LETTER

"We have read your manuscript with boundless delight. If we were to publish your paper, however, it would then be impossible for us to publish any work of a lower standard. And it is unthinkable that in the next thousand years we shall see its equal. We are, to our regret, compelled to return your divine composition and to beg you one thousand times to overlook our short-sighted timidity."

Westerners are amused by this letter and immediately say that it doesn't correspond to their mindset. Why not? Westerners and Asians may share a common experience when confronted with the notions of "rejection" and "saving face", but these notions are perceived by each as "a kaleidoscopic flux of impressions that has to be organized by our mind —and this means mostly by the linguistic system of our mind."

Because "saving face" is critical to survival and deeply embedded in the Asian mental pathways, the Chinese possess a formidable number of honorific expressions, as they appear in the letter above. In American culture, where "saving face" is considerably less important, it is hardly expressed at all because it doesn't have the required vocabulary. Essentially, our language acts as a continual conditioner of reality, preventing us from considering completely new values or mental approaches.

"The Awful German Language"

One can learn much about thinking and perception in a culture through the study of its language. That is exactly what Mark Twain did back in 1879 while learning German in Heidelberg. In his humorous essay entitled "The Awful German Language", he writes that a person who has not studied German has no idea of what a perplexing language it is. Some excerpts:

German sentence structure: An average sentence, in a German newspaper, is a sublime and impressive curiosity; it occupies a quarter of a column; it contains all the ten parts of speech — not in regular order, but mixed; it is built mainly of compound words constructed by the writer on the spot, and not to be found in any dictionary — six or seven words compacted into one, without joint or seam — that is, without hyphens; it treats of fourteen or fifteen subjects, each enclosed in a parenthesis of its own with here and there extra parentheses...: finally, all the parentheses and re-parentheses are massed together between a couple of king-parentheses, one of which is placed in the first line of the majestic sentence and the other in the middle of the last line of it — after which comes the verb, and you find out for the first time what the man has been talking about; and after the verb — merely by way of ornament, so far as I can make out — the writer shovels in "*haben sind gewesen gehabt haben geworden sein,*" or words to that effect, and the monument is finished.

Mark Twain

Verb placement: You observe [in German sentences] how far that verb is from the reader's base of operations; well, in a German newspaper they put their verb away over on the next page; and I have heard that sometimes after stringing along the exciting preliminaries and parentheses for a column or two, they get in a hurry and have to go to press without getting to the verb at all. Of course, then, the reader is left in a very exhausted and ignorant state.

Personal pronouns: Personal pronouns and adjectives are a fruitful nuisance in this language, and should have been left out. For instance, the same sound, *sie*, means *you*, and it means *she*, and it means *her*, and it means *it*, and it means *they*, and it means *them*. Think of the ragged poverty of a language which has to make one word do the work of six — and a poor little weak thing of only three letters at that. But mainly, think of the exasperation of never knowing which of these meanings the speaker is trying to convey. This explains why, whenever a person says *sie* to me, I generally try to kill him, if a stranger.

Non-Verbal Behavior

Communicating in a foreign culture is not only using the culture's verbal code. Equally important is non-verbal behavior. According to research, some 80 to 90% of what we communicate is the result of non-verbal messages, what anthropologists refer to as "hidden signals". They can be eye contact, facial expression, touch, posture, tone and tempo of voice, attitude, clothing artifacts. These subtle signals can baffle the uninitiated and cause communication breakdowns.

Non-verbal repertoires are learned directly, either through active observation or personal experiences. If the non-verbal codes are violated, members of the culture will most often attribute it to aspects of personality, attitudes or intelligence.

The following demonstrates how misunderstandings occur when people are unaware of their counterpart's gestures.

> Johann Schneider, a purchaser for a large German pharmaceutical compay-flies to London to negotiate with a certain Charles Grant of a British chemical company. After the negotiations have been in progress for 20 minutes, Charles begins to relax in his executive chair. Johann, who is sitting upright and very attentive, feels that Charles is not respecting him and becomes aggressive. Charles doesn't understand Johann's sudden change in behavior and asks himself "Is this a negotiating tactic to get a better price?"

In German culture, people are taught to be serious and credible when communicating. The upright position of Johann signals that he's taking the negotiations earnestly. In British culture, emphasis is placed first on the relationship, then business. Charles thinks it would be a good idea to take a relaxed position in order to lighten the situation. Because the two men don't understand the other person's non-verbal signals, the negotiation takes a turn for the worse.

Here's another example of how motivation can be wrongly judged through body language.

> The management of a large multinational American company was astonished by the extraordinary results of the research and development department in their German subsidiary. Wanting to know the secrets of their success, they sent over a delegation to find out about the "magical ways of the Germans".

> After one week of questioning and observation, the American team wrote in their report that they couldn't discover any patterns and were furthermore perplexed by their Germans colleagues, who appeared to have "no drive". Upon learning the conclusion of the study, the angry German staff demanded an immediate revision of the report.

The delegation came with American notions of success, which meant looking for "pro-active" and "always on the go" physical movements. For Germans, success was obtained through quiet reflection and analysis before any activity was undertaken.

Or consider the following example of grief:

> In a scene in an American film, college students in Los Angeles are having dinner. One is suddenly called to the phone and learns that her mother has just died. Upon putting the phone down, she remains still for a moment, and then proceeds to inform the others of the nature of the call, politely excuses herself from the group to leave. Viewers of the movie perceive her behavior differently according to their cultural background. Italians and Greek think: "She is so insincere; she doesn't even cry". Poles and Russians say: "Why didn't she share her sadness with her friends". And the reaction of Americans: "How courageous; she just wants to bear her sadness by herself."

Another form of non-verbal behavior is *touch* (haptics); where, how and how often people touch each other differs across cultures. In the US, if a male employee were to unintentionally touch his female office assistant on the shoulder, it could be grounds for a sexual harassment law suit. In France, males kissing each other on the cheeks as a form of greeting is considered perfectly normal behavior, to the astonishment of Americans.

The tone of voice, speed and pitch, known as *paralanguage*, can convey different messages. A short, terse "come in" strongly suggests "I really don't want to see you" whereas a moderate, drawn out "come in" indicates a welcome.

All these examples illustrate how non-verbal language is used to add, reinforce, or replace the verbal-code system. More importantly, we can see how greatly cultures differ in their interpretations.

Perception

Perception is at the core of intercultural communication. It is the process by which we select, organize, and evaluate stimuli from the outside world so that we can create mental experiences within ourselves. We tend to assume that we all perceive reality in basically the same way. Whatever I say, see or do will have the same meaning to others as it does to me. But even people who share many common values and experiences, misperceive, misinterpret and misevaluate each other's realities. When we are in a foreign culture, the chances of culturally correct perception are reduced even further.

For example, Americans with their strong Puritan background are generally surprised to find nudity on European prime time television and perceive it as something that should not be seen. To a typical European, nudity is just part of life and generally the display of the nude body is not disturbing. However, these very same Europeans perceive the Americans' boundless need to smile as odd and and artificial, whereas for Americans smiling is considered a natural part of life.

"The soul... never thinks without a picture."
– Aristotle

These two examples point out that pure perceptional objectivity is not possible because it is, in fact, neither absolute nor innate. It is learned and part of our cultural experience. People who say that Europeans are sexually immoral or that Americans are superficial are rarely doing this with intentional malice. Instead, their thoughts simply reflect culturally based biases. Lack of awareness of this phenomenon generally leads to a communication breakdown and the sometimes patronizing need to "correct" others.

Our limited capacity to perceive people and situations means we need to develop new strategies to overcome our natural parochial tendencies. When working in a foreign environment, the best policy to reduce premature judgments is to stress description rather than interpretation or evaluation (see pages 105-6). Effective cross-cultural awareness rejects the dominance of one reality over another, encouraging instead the equal interplay of alternative realities.

Exercise

Perceiving Non-Verbal Behavior

Leonardo da Vinci's Mona Lisa is one of the most intriguing figures in art history. Yet, many people ask what it is that makes her so appealing. The answer is her discreet, mysterious smile. It is exactly this non-verbal behavior, functioning at a subconscious level, which has remained an enigma to this day.

Art experts tell us that to get to the essence of this painting, you need to put aside your analytical mind and let your spirit flow into the smile. Those who have tried this have responded with the following perceptions:

> "When I smile like that, I have a feeling of liberty inside me."
> "I perceived a sudden transformation — my perspective of things was suddenly different."
> "I feel she's smiling at me."
> "I have this paradoxical feeling of being in two places at once."
> "I feel I'm being thrown back into the quiet period of the Renaissance."

Meditate on Mona Lisa's smile for a few minutes, incorporating her into your soul. Does your thinking change when you look from her perspective?

The purpose of this exercise is to point out how perception (often unconsciously) selects, organizes and evaluates stimuli, which in turn create mental experiences within ourselves. And as we become more conscious of how perception is determined mostly by our cultural experience, we can learn to free ourselves from limiting thought and action. This awareness alone is an important skill in intercultural relations.

Exercise

How Non-Americans Perceive Americans

Some years ago, *Newsweek* asked people in six countries — Brazil, France, Great Britain, Japan, Mexico and Germany — how they perceived Americans. They were shown a list of qualities given at the bottom of the page and asked to choose those they associated most and least with Americans.

Before you look up the responses, do the same with the list of qualities.

What do you think were the four qualities most associated with Americans?

1. ____________________ 2. ____________________

3. ____________________ 4. ____________________

What do you think were the four qualities least associated with Americans?

1. ____________________ 2. ____________________

3. ____________________ 4. ____________________

QUALITIES

Decisive	***Energetic***	***Honest***
Industrious	***Sexy***	***Self-indulgent***
Sophisticated	***Intelligent***	***Friendly***
Greedy	***Nationalistic***	***Inventive***
Lazy	***Rude***	

Now compare your perceptions with the survey results from *Newsweek* on page 138

PERCEPTUAL PATTERNS

1. Quickly read the following three sentences below.

ONCE	PARIS	BIRD
IN A	IN THE	IN THE
A LIFETIME.	THE SPRING.	THE HAND.

Few of you will have seen the double articles in each sentence. We've skipped the "a"s and "the"s because our cognitive maps are programmed to know that they aren't important for our understanding. As a result, our perceptual filters prevent us from seeing what we don't expect to see.

2. Read the following sentence and quickly count the number of Fs.

FINISHED FILES ARE THE RESULT OF YEARS OF SCIENTIFIC STUDY COMBINED WITH THE EXPERIENCE OF YEARS.

If your mother tongue is English, you'll most likely have counted only three Fs. If you are a non-native speaker, you'll most likely have counted all six *Fs*. Why? Native English speakers will automatically read the sentence (a natural activity), and at the same time count the *Fs* (an unnatural activity). We unconsciously select only those words that are important according to our cultural conditioning. This means we skip the three ***of***s simply because prepositions *are* not important for understanding. Once we develop the habit of reading in a certain way, we usually continue to read/see it in that way. Again, our perceptual filters impede us from dealing properly with reality.

These two exercises teach an important lesson on how perceptual patterns are shaped. Whether it's about reading sentences or interpreting other people's behavior, perceptions are learned, culturally determined, consistent, and often inaccurate.

Stereotyping

A stereotype is a form of mental categorization or "thinking shortcut" that helps describe the characteristics or tendencies of a particular group or people. Contrary to general opinion, *everyone* stereotypes.

To illustrate how it works, imagine the particular characteristics of each of the following: Brazilians, California surfers, factory workers, French gendarmes, housewives. Now, let's assume one person from one of these categories walks into the room and begins talking to you. Most likely, you will attribute the stereotype's traits you just imagined to that specific individual.

Why is this so? Our minds are bombarded with more stimuli than we can handle, which then leads us to "pigeon-hole". The human mind cannot resist putting people and things into categories; it's an attempt to find order in a chaotic and confusing world. This, in a nutshell, is why we create national and ethnic caricatures.

Stereotyping describes a group norm, not the specific characteristics of an individual. A particular Russian might resemble a certain American, but a Russian orchestra or a volleyball team is clearly perceived differently from its American counterpart.

Most often stereotyping carries a negative connotation. At home, school and work, we're repeatedly told not to stereotype because it's considered to be primitive thinking, unsophisticated, "politically incorrect". It's also unethical: stereotypes can become a problem when they are used to evaluate people as good or bad. Statements such as "Blacks are ...", "Muslims are not..." or "Women should..." often foster counterproductive attitudes and behaviors because they are based on half-truths or distortions.

However, stereotypes are not always necessarily erroneous. They can be positive when they reduce behavioral complexity to manageable proportions. For instance, Canadians might say the French write elegantly, the British are witty, and the Chinese are entrepreneurial.

Yet, a "positive" value may, in fact, be perceived as a negative trait by a person from another country. Someone brought up in a very structured and organized social system, such as Germany, might belittle the French as spending too much time on writing flowery phrases, the British as never serious, the Chinese as gaining market shares unfairly by any means.

This brings us to a cardinal rule: what is positive behavior in one culture may be viewed as negative in another one. In another words, throughout the world there are infinite ways of doing things, most of which are neither better nor worse than our own, but are simply different.

Sensitive people are intuitively aware of this and make it their continual habit to observe cultural diversity without judging it. They actively use stereotypes as an initial guide for understanding foreign behavior and, if need be, modify the stereotype when actual observations and experience prove them otherwise.

Researcher Indre Ratiu in collaboration with the business school INSEAD in France and the London Business School found that the managers identified as "most internationally effective" are those who alter their stereotypes if faced with contradictory evidence. Managers characterized as "least internationally effective"

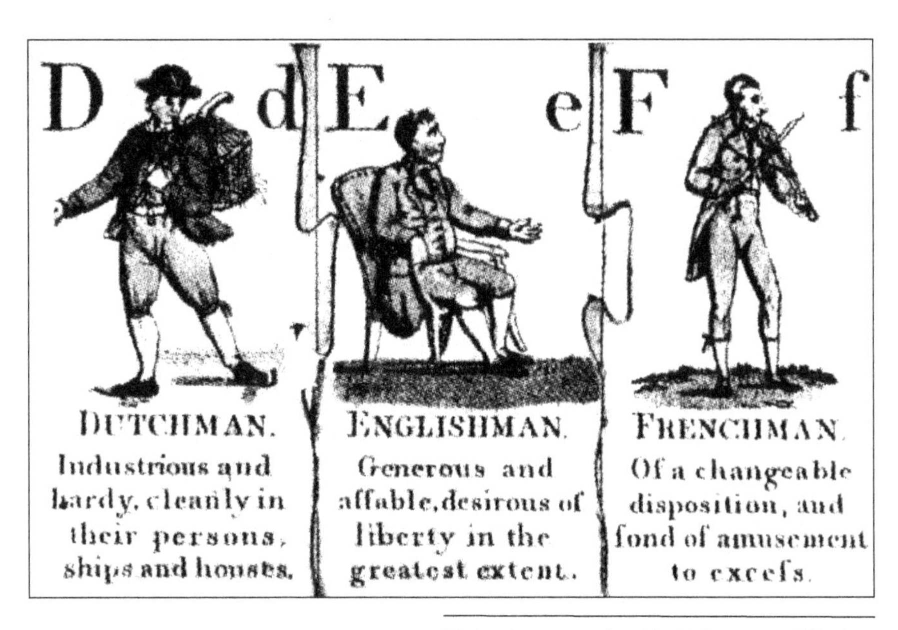

National stereotypes found in 18th century publications

> "... when your thinking rises above concern for your own welfare, wisdom which is independent of thought appears."
>
> – Ha Gakure (*Hidden Leaves*)

maintain stereotypes even when presented with conflicting information, refusing to get to the richer reality which was lying beyond them.

Stereotyping can specifically reinforce self-fulfilling prophecies. Researchers at Princeton University did the following experiment. They arbitrarily chose 60 undergraduate males, 30 white, 30 black. The young men were randomly separated into two groups, each containing 15 whites and 15 blacks. In the first group, the young men were each asked to play a round of mini-golf. The researchers told them they were studying the correlation between physical coordination and actual playing. The second group, likewise, was asked to play a round of mini-golf. However, the researchers told them, they were observing if a good score could be correlated between mental strategy and actual playing. When the results were tabulated, the blacks in the first group scored on average significantly better than the whites, whereas in the second group, the whites did better than the blacks.

Why was there such a difference? In the United States, floating in the collective unconscious is the stereotypical idea that when it comes to athletic abilities, blacks are far superior to whites. At the same time, there is the belief that when it comes to strategy, whites always outperform blacks. The researchers effectively demonstrated that by evoking certain stereotypical images, you can motivate or de-motivate a person's own internal self-esteem.

This is an important point to remember when abroad. There will be times when you will be *personally* held responsible for the stereotype you appear to represent. How do you respond if someone says: "You are such an insensitive perfectionist", "You are so wasteful.", "You Americans have no culture."

Either you can fulfill the other person's image of you or do what experienced expatriates have discovered to be the best counter-measure:

- Resist becoming angry or defensive.
- Refrain from fulfilling negative stereotypes.
- Persist in being a pleasant (charming) person.
- Attempt to let your real personality emerge.

OBSERVATIONS OF DIFFERENT COUNTRIES

Here is a selection of observations of different countries, made either by foreign visitors or citizens of the country in question. Take the time to ask yourself if each observation is accurate. How would you explain the trait in question?

- **Germans on the British:** "The British never come out with an honest statement. It might be sizzling hot and they'll say with a perfectly straight face "It's a bit warm, isn't it?"

- **French on the French:** "The French are at once the most brilliant and the most dangerous of all European nations, and the best qualified to become, in the eyes of other peoples, an object of admiration, of hatred, of compassion — never of indifference."

- **French on the Americans:** "Americans make bad coffee and have no capacity for abstract thought."

- **Austrians on Austrians:** "Austrians draw a good deal of their strength from this idea of the middle, of the center, of the compromise, exhibiting an almost narcissistic love of the middle way and a leveling of extremes."

- **Italians on Italians:** "In Italy information tends to be processed subjectively; Italians will look at the particulars of each situation rather than appeal to a law or rule to solve a problem."

- **British on the Chinese:** "China sees herself as *Chung-Kuo* — the center of the universe and culturally superior to foreigners, who are viewed as inferior, corrupt, decadent, disloyal, barbaric and, in essence, 'devils'."

- **Americans on Germans:** "Germans have a penchant for coming to meetings armed with tons of overhead transparencies and colored charts. It's absolute information overkill."

- **Canadians on Brazilians:** "Brazilians actually believe that it's impolite to arrive at someone's house for dinner on time; being 30 minutes to 45 minutes late is the norm."

Ethnocentrism

One of the biggest impediments to intercultural communication is ethnocentrism, the belief that the values and assumptions of one's culture are superior to those of other cultures. The term originates from the Greek word *ethnos*, meaning "nation". It is defined as viewing one's own group as the center of everything, and evaluating all others according to the standards of one's own culture.

Ethnocentrism is a primordial desire and serves as a basic survival strategy by linking us to the group. It teaches us that our culture is "right" or "correct," and those who do not accept our values are wrong. The ethnocentric feeling explains why the Greeks and Romans called outsiders "barbarians". Likewise Arabs considered themselves as the noblest nation and all others as barbarians. In the 19th century Americans, inspired by the motto "Manifest Destiny", saw themselves as a "chosen people". The Jews divide all mankind into themselves and Gentiles — they being the "chosen people". The Chinese and Japanese have regarded themselves as the "center" of the universe. As do the French, Russians, Egyptians and everybody else.

As it is the ageless human habit of seeking similarity, then it's no wonder that ethnocentrism produces emotional reactions that decrease people's willingness to understand other cultures. A conscious awareness of our ethnocentric impulses will minimize initial hostilities and in the end enable us to interact more fluidly and successfully with other nationalities.

Food For Thought

Intercultural sensitivity is not natural. By nature, we seek similarity, people like ourselves. It's a natural product of our tribal instinct, part of our primate past. If you look back at history, you will find that cross-cultural encounters have mostly been characterized by bloodshed, oppression and even genocide. If contact was made with "strangers", it was usually for reasons of trade or/and war.

Now in this age of globalization, we are suddenly told that our unconscious natural habits of protecting our tribe and living in splendid isolation have become dysfunctional. We are expected to live and work in harmony with other groups. To say that most of us haven't been prepared is more than an understatement — it mirrors the difficulty of overcoming our ethnocentric instinct.

DISCOVERING ETHNOCENTRISM

Below are eight statements.

— Place an "a" or "d" beside each statement to indicate whether you personally agree (a) or disagree (d).
— If you disagree with one, change the wording so that the statement is acceptable, as reworded, to you.
— You may not simply "agree to disagree".
— The suggested changes and explanations you will find on page 138.

1. The fact that the first automobile was invented by Gottlieb Daimler is proof of the technological superiority of Germans.

2. Asians do many things backwards.

3. The Arabs who flew the passenger jets into the World Trade Center did not value human life; to them life is cheap.

4. Primitive people have not yet reached the higher stages of civilization.

5. Minority members of a population should conform to the customs and values of the majority.

6. Americans have absolutely no culture.

7. If other nations were as orderly and punctual as the Germans, the world would be a much better place and people everywhere would treat each other better.

8. Everyone should learn English as it is the one unifying language.

Culture Shock

The term was first coined in 1955 by the anthropologist Klavero Oberg to describe the psychological disorientation Americans experienced when adjusting to work on a health project in Brazil. He defined it as "an occupational disease of people who have suddenly been transported abroad and is precipitated by the anxiety that results from losing all familiar signs and symbols of social interaction".

Synonyms are homesickness, uprootedness and adjustment difficulties. It's not some sort of illness (which many people imagine it to be), rather it's a learning experience and a natural phenomenon when adjusting to a foreign culture. For some, it will be brief and hardly an upheaval. For others, it is a trying period of psychological stress that can be of a long duration. Those who are exposed to culture shock and overcome it are more psychologically sound, more stable than before.

Someone who claims to have never experienced it is either fairly unaware of his or her own feelings or has never adjusted cross-culturally. Tourists who remain within their national group generally don't experience culture shock.

There are four stages of culture shock and the whole time span varies from a few months to possibly a year or more, depending on the duration spent abroad:

1. ***honeymoon stage***: characterized by euphoria; everything in the new country seems new and exotic.
2. ***horror stage***: characterized by rejection of the new country; frustration, disorientation and helplessness.
3. ***humor stage***: characterized by reflection; laughter at past mistakes in the new country, now feeling oneself on the road to recovery.
4. ***home stage***: back to normalcy with the ability to function in two cultures; feeling in control of one's life and destiny.

The fundamental cause of culture shock is due to the loss of familiar cues, i.e. the breakdown of interpersonal communication. Everyone is surrounded by thousands of physical and social signals, present since childhood, which provide a sense of identity in subtle, indirect ways. Their absence makes you feel like "a fish out of water". Behavior is no longer clearly right or wrong, but ambiguous. In a new culture, "good morning", "thank you," and "how are you?" may no longer bring the response we're accustomed to. It's not even clear when we should smile or laugh. These simple gestures don't seem to elicit the cues we need.

Culture shock is like being a fish out of water.

The resulting reaction is frustration and anger which we usually irrationally displace onto those whom we perceive to be lower in the social hierarchy (taxi drivers, waiters, porters, secretaries). Repeated negative experiences of disorientation can lead to a form of "learned helplessness", alienation.

People going through culture shock are often not aware that this adjustment to the new environment can be painful. An animal experiencing pain reacts by fleeing the source of that pain (avoidance behavior) or by displaying aggression (fight behavior). Humans also have "fight or flight" tendencies, but usually distort, simplify or deny the complex reality of the painful situation. Ultimately, people lose their center and cannot find alternative ways of behaving. Instead of acting, they end up reacting.

The most common symptoms of culture shock are lack of control and hopelessness, i.e. boredom, withdrawal, the need for excessive amounts of sleep, compulsive eating or drinking, sterotyping and hostility toward host nationals.

The best way of overcoming culture shock is simply understanding what the process of cross-cultural adjustment is. Culture shock is a normal reaction which does, in fact, end — sooner or later. While this explanation offers no specific answers, it does help the expatriate replace stress and frustration with coping strategies.

Reverse Culture Shock: Upon returning home, one may find oneself experiencing the "fifth" phase of culture shock — "re-entry shock". The expatriate may have become comfortable with the habits and customs of a new lifestyle and no longer feel at ease in the home culture. Additionally, the person may feel unappreciated and unwanted at work and view his/her countrymen as spoiled, materialistic and wasteful. Re-entry shock can be minimized by first understanding that it's a natural occurrence. The irritation — hopelessness, wanting to get back — will resolve itself with time and result in a more solid outlook on life.

ADVICE

COPING WITH CULTURE SHOCK

While accepting the fact that culture shock will mean a certain inescapable period of despondency, there are nevertheless steps that can be taken to reduce the impact. Here are points you can think about and act upon:

1. Become conscious of the fact that culture shock is a natural occurrence for anybody who plans to live abroad for a substantial period of time. Realizing that it's human and natural to be frustrated, angry, confused and lost when coming to grips with new surroundings helps considerably from a psychological point of view.

2. Culture shock is a great teacher in telling us how we are all prisoners of our own cultural upbringing. It is only when faced with other ways of doing things that we gain the insight and wisdom that our own culture is not the only possessor of knowledge, the best way or the ultimate source of happiness. The "shock" of becoming conscious of this, painful though it may be, can ironically become a form of liberation!

3. Learn to be patient. When you are living and working in a new culture where previous learning no longer applies, it is going to take some time for the psyche to adapt.

4. Be positive and constructive when in an unfavorable situation. Avoid comparing, criticizing, complaining. Remember that this is a learning experience which will make you stronger and more solid in the long run.

5. Begin to consciously examine the logical reasons behind the behaviors of your host culture. Studies have shown that the best adjusted expatriates are those who continually ask themselves why their foreign counterparts are acting the way they do. Search for patterns and the pieces that fit together. This sort of mental detective work often results in positive and even essential insights about others and yourself.

6. Acquire knowledge about the new culture through books, brochures, local ethnic cooking. Start learning the language, or at least try to acquire a basic understanding of it. And increase contact with the new culture — volunteer in community activities that allow you to come in contact with host nationals.

7. Stay in contact with your cultural group; not only people-wise, but also through newspapers, TV, internet, e-mail. This will somewhat alleviate the feeling of homesickness and alienation. Seek a fellow countryman who has been there longer and has a positive attitude to the country. You can use that person as a sounding board when feeling anxious and confused.

8. Avoid other compatriots and those foreigners who refuse to deal with culture shock and have nothing better to do than make disparaging remarks and jokes about the "stupid natives". They are essentially seeking others to confirm that their negative assessment of the host country is right. This negative attitude can be quite contagious, leading to a further vicious cycle of frustration.

9. Focus on how you really feel — what is really going on inside you and not what you think is wrong with your host culture. Allow yourself to feel sad about the things that you have left behind: your family, your friends, your security zone. At the same time, draw up a list of positive things in your present situation. The act of counterbalancing the positive with the negative will in many instances provide perspective and a more realistic appraisal of your present situation.

10. And lastly, try to keep a healthy sense of humor. You will be making foolish mistakes that may cause you embarrassment, but it will pass. Some years later, you will look back at these awkward events with a smile and realize that it was, actually, a wonderful learning experience.

III

Compe

Competence

Strategies for Overcoming Misunderstandings

We have up to now examined definitions and models of culture and communication, as well as barriers that can lead to communication breakdowns. After realizing that we aren't aware of everything, that our intuitions may be wrong and uncertainty remains, we then understand why intercultural competence is a necessity. This section provides practical techniques and strategies, new ways of perceiving the human condition for better communication across cultures.

It would be, however, useful to stop for a moment and reflect why we seek to reduce misunderstandings. Interculturalist Richard Brislin provides a critical thought:

> *"It is to call upon the skill that separates us from other primates: we can think about and reflect upon our behavior. We can become aware of ethnocentric thinking, intercept ourselves when putting culturally diverse others at a disadvantage and switch to a more tolerant and culturally relevant position."*

KNOW YOUR HOST'S BACKGROUND, COUNTRY AND CULTURE

Actively seeking information about people or cultures other than your own can help counter inaccurate information and prejudice and reduce uncertainty and anxiety.

Discovering how much you think you know about the person or country is important. Be curious and make inquiries. Most people are eager to tell visitors about their country. The following questions will assist you in your investigation. Obviously, some of these questions should remain as speculations in your own mind.

Family profile:

How large is the person's family? How many brothers and sisters does that person have?
What is the economic status of the family? Did the family earn or inherit its wealth?
Does the person belong to a religious group? Does it affect the person's behavior?
What sort of education has the person received?
Is that person married? Does the person have children?
What are the person's deepest values?
What's the person career? Why did that person choose it?

Host country:

What are the facts about the country you are going to, such as history, geography, climate, major cities, transportation system, etc.?
How is the family structured?
What are the important customs (birth, marriage, death, etc.) and courtesies?
What are the religious and philosophical beliefs, proverbs and superstitions?
How is the education system set up?
In school, what pedagogical approaches are used?
What are the cultural achievements in the arts?
What are the country's major industries, exports, imports?
Does it have a major agriculture industry?
What sort of drink and food do people consume?
What type of government is practiced?
How are the police and military organized?
What sports are played? What sort of games do children learn?
What languages, local dialects are spoken?

Cultural Background:

What thoughts come to mind when the host culture is mentioned?
What do you want to learn about the host culture?
What does your interlocutor like / dislike about your culture?
What do you like / dislike about the host culture?
What are the advantages / disadvantages of living in the host culture?

UNDERSTANDING OTHERS

In this remarkable passage from his essay *Visit to America*, Jawaharlal Nehru, India's first Prime Minister, writes his views on what a person needs to understand others.

If we seek to understand a people, we have to try to put ourselves, as far as we can, in that particular historical and cultural background... It is not easy for a person of one country to enter into the background of another country. So there is great irritation, because one fact that seems obvious to us is not immediately accepted by the other party or does not seem obvious to him at all ... But that extreme irritation will go when we think... that he is just differently conditioned and simply can't get out of that condition.

One has to recognize that whatever the future may hold, countries and people differ... in their approach to life and their ways of living and thinking. In order to understand them, we have to understand their way of life and approach.

If we wish to convince them, we have to use their language as far as we can, not language in the narrow sense of the word, but the language of the mind. That is one necessity. Something that goes even further than that is not the appeal to logic and reason, but some kind of emotional awareness of other people.

Prime Minister Nehru shaking hands with President Eisenhower during his visit to the USA in 1956.

DEVELOPING LISTENING AS A SKILL

When you meet a person from another culture, a simple and effective technique for gathering information is to ask questions, then pause to listen. This technique also provides clues on how values and assumptions are affecting their perceptions and behaviors.

Most people, unfortunately, have a hard time listening. Much miscommunication occurs because people aren't listening actively or are only listening to the words, not the meaning.

Try the following experiment: find someone you don't know too well — a colleague, a neighbor or perhaps the postman. Tell that person you wish to discuss for two minutes a subject of importance to you (music, children, a scandal etc). After listening for two minutes, ask your listener to summarize as accurately as possible what you said. If it is inaccurate in any way, correct it and ask for a re-summary. What you'll discover is that people have a difficult time recapitulating what you said exactly.

And when you add non-verbal messages that are often different in a foreign culture, it's no wonder that misunderstandings frequently occur.

To overcome this, there is a method that astute people use: ask your interlocutor what he or she exactly means. It's as simple as that. Linguists call this process "perception-checking". Likewise, when you are making an important point, you may ask them to put it in their own words to check comprehension.

Additionally, be ready to share information about yourself.

Listening attentively to what the other person has said has been an ageless problem as this 19th century French gravure wonderfully depicts.

This permits your counterpart to gain fresh perspectives about you and may modify his or her behavior and outlook. Otherwise, your interlocutor might feel you are just like an interrogator wishing to gain power and dominate rather than have a sincere desire to understand.

A few other points: when your partners are speaking, but not in their native language, encourage them verbally and non-verbally. This helps psychologically. Also, take more breaks, as second-language communication is exhausting.

Lastly, repeat each important idea, using different words to explain the same concept. Often, it takes time and several exchanges to clarify a message in a foreign culture. The rule here is to be patient and learn to expand your capacity to tolerate ambiguity.

DESCRIPTION, INTERPRETATION, EVALUATION

This is a relatively simple tool that widens your choices for analyzing why we react and behave the way we do in a new culture. Normally, when people see, hear and receive information from their environment, almost all persons immediately interpret and judge it without being conscious of the sensory impact.

For instance, you land at Cape Town airport in South Africa for the first time and take a taxi into the city. On the way, you see nothing but sterile, dull, block-like buildings. It wouldn't come to your mind to say: "The buildings are twenty meters high, walls are of a dull brown color and have twenty-four windows per side". Rather, you are likely to make the following comment: "How ugly and drab. These South Africans have no taste for fine architecture". Rarely do we realize that our interpretation and judgment are based on unconscious projections of our own cultural preferences.

It's possible to train the mind to distinguish between *observation, interpretation* and *evaluation.* It allows you to suspend judgment and consider alternative hypothesis or interpretation. A statement of observation describes the specific perceptual cues and sensory information without judgment or interpretations, i.e. without being deformed by opinion. Police officers are trained to do this when reporting an accident or crime. This is also the basic rule for any proper intercultural encounter.

Read the following and note how different observations, interpretations and evaluations affect the intercultural competence of Wong, a young Chinese executive starting work in the United States. He writes to his parents about his first experiences at work:

> When I arrived at my office, my new supervisor met me. He asked me to call him by his first name, Bob. I was surprised, but that wasn't the most shocking part. As we were talking in his office, he put his feet on his desk. I knew Americans were casual, but his behavior was ridiculous, completely out of line. I felt insulted and offended by his attitude.

If Wong had analyzed the puzzling behavior of Bob by separating his observation, interpreting and evaluations, he may have come to different conclusions.

Descriptive statements might be:

- American managers ask to be called by their first names
- They sometimes put their feet on the desk

The sensory information could be *interpreted* in the following manner:

- First names are said to everyone
- Americans don't like being called by their family name
- In the USA, it's a custom to put your feet on the table
- Americans like to show how relaxed they are by putting feet on the desk
- Americans exercise their legs, even when sitting at the desk

Because there are many interpretations, it increases your options for *evaluations*:

- Americans like to put everyone at ease and I am actually enjoying this casual way of meeting people for the first time.
- I don't like calling my supervisors by their first names and having to put up with their laid-back attitude. I will remain polite because my aim is to be well regarded and hope it will help me be promoted.

NON-CONVENTIONAL SKILLS FOR OVERSEAS SUCCESS

When asked about the skills necessary for international work, personnel managers list attitudes such as empathy, openness, communicativeness, flexibility, perceptiveness and so on. It sounds logical and they base their selection of people on it.

On the other hand, Robert Kohls, former director of the Washington International Center and author of *Survival Kit for Overseas Living* (considered a classic among intercultural trainers), mentions three other important traits which are rarely thought of.

The first is a *sense of humor.* No matter how well you're prepared for your assignment, there will be moments of anger, annoyance, discouragement and embarrassment. The best defense is the ability to laugh things off.

Being less task-driven is the second trait. Managers are chosen for foreign assignments because they're the company's stars or because they've been given a specific project. They set extremely high goals for themselves and those they supervise to reach within a stipulated period. However, "unspoken rules" must first be learned, then mastered.The same behavioral traits may not work in the new culture and certainly not in the same way. Expatriates less concerned with winning at all costs tend to be more effective and better able to enjoy their experience.

Closely related is the *ability to tolerate failure,* the third trait. The executive selected to go abroad has normally gone from success to success in the corporate world. But anyone who's been overseas for a few years will tell you that nobody comes back with a perfect record. Setbacks are part of the adaptation process, as is a certain amount of frustration.

> "Stately towers tumble down with a heavier crash than more lowly buildings."
> – HORACE

These "unorthodox" ideas almost always encounter some resistance in seminars, especially from those in the personnel department. Once they are bounced around, however, initial critics usually become the biggest supporters. Many of the savvier companies and institutions are now adding "a sense of humor", "less driven" and "the ability to fail" to their expatriate selection criteria.

SYMPATHY AND EMPATHY

Interculturalist Milton Bennett has written on how feelings of sympathy and empathy can affect intercultural communication. He argues strongly that knowing and understanding the difference between them is a pre-requisite to developing cultural competence.

He begins with the "golden rule": treat other people the way you want to be treated by them. This, in fact, denies that people are different. It assumes that people are only different in the outer layers of culture, such as behavior, manners and style and deep down, we are essentially the same, sharing the same strivings and values. This assumption is very closely related to that of ethnocentrism, the tendency to see our own culture as the center of the universe.

If one follows the "golden rule", communication strategy is based on sympathy, which he defines as "the imaginative placing of ourselves in another person's position". He explains further, "We are not here imagining how the other person thinks or feels, but rather we are referencing how *we* ourselves might think or feel in similar circumstances." A simple example is if I tell you that my dog recently died, you might sympathize by "imagining" how you would feel (or have felt) about your dog dying.

However, if we accept the premise that each human being is essentially unique, with distinct psychological patterns, individual language and cultural differences, the golden rule of similarity can lead to a breakdown in communications. In the above example, a person with a Muslim upbringing would probably demonstrate no sympathy because a dog in the Muslim culture is considered as unclean and unholy.

> "If there was less sympathy in the world, there would be less trouble in the world."
> — Oscar Wilde

To avoid such misunderstandings, Bennett urges a strategy of empathy, which he defines as "the imaginative intellectual and emotional participation in another person's experience."

Going further, Bennett says "we need to get inside the head and heart of the other, to participate in his or her experience as if we were really the other person". This means, we let our self-boundary go and emotionally "pick up" people's

Reaching out, acknowledging and respecting each person's uniqueness is the basis of empathy, as portrayed metaphorically in Gustave Courbet's painting Bonjour.

thoughts and feelings (vibrations) from their own perspective. An example is when a friend tells you that he was bypassed for a promotion, you can "participate" in his/her feelings of disappointment.

Essentially, the difference between sympathy and empathy is one of perspectives. Sympathy is based on the assumption and perspective that all human beings are deep down the same, whereas empathy shifts perspectives and takes the inner position that each person is unique. Successful communication should be approached as if each person is different and the differences should be acknowledged and respected. Bennett summarizes by formulating a "platinum rule": "Be aware of how others would like to be treated from their own perspective."

"Earthly things must be known to be loved; divine things must be loved to be known."
– Blaise Pascal

MOVING TOWARD A "THIRD CULTURE" REALITY

When people find that their cultural differences are blocking communication, a new strategy is called for. In the ideal situation, all parties would strive to create a shared "third culture" reality by first becoming conscious of the fact that different values and perspectives are causing misunderstandings. This implies that all involved would have already gained an awareness of themselves and their cultural values and how it is affecting face-to-face interaction. Additionally, there would be a positive will to accommodate, understand and appreciate cultural differences.

> "If you see in any given situation only what everybody else can see, you can be said to be so much a representative of your culture that you are a victim of it."
>
> – S. I. HAYAKAWA

If these three points are present, new mental frameworks and feelings can emerge, permitting a different form of communication. There would be a willingness to suspend old ways in order to temporarily expand and experiment into new areas.

It's a dynamic process where the communicators are continuously conscious of their own cultural boundaries, but parallel to that, allow themselves to expand and wander into the other person's mind. This "other" perspective, more commonly known as empathy, permits events to be reconstructed in different contexts to generate alternative cultural experiences.

Mahatma Ghandi perhaps expressed the "third culture" reality best: "There is a place beyond right and wrong. I'll meet you there." For him, this meeting place is where there's a total absence of criticism, value judgements, analysis and blaming.

As experienced expatriates will tell you, intercultural effectiveness depends largely on building working and social relationships with your counterpart. Finding out what expectations your host has of you as well as getting across your expectations through empathy is a means of creating trust and demonstrating your sincerity and goodwill. It is, in the end, the universal way to reach out and establish connections with all peoples. (*for more on this, see page 65 — constructivist communication*)

DEVELOPMENTAL MODEL OF INTERCULTURAL SENSITIVITY

We learned earlier that culture shock is a disorientation that can occur when trying to adapt to a different cultural setting. It is a relatively simple description of cultural adaptation. A richer and more satisfying account of cultural adaptation is the *Developmental Model of Intercultural Sensitivity* (DMIS) from interculturalist Milton Bennett. This theoretical framework, first published in 1986, is considered by the majority of intercultural professionals as the most complete explanation of what an individual goes through to develop intercultural competence.

In both the academic and corporate worlds, Dr. Bennett observed that individuals confronted cultural difference in predictable ways as they acquired more intercultural sensitivity. He organized these observations into six stages of increasing sensitivity to cultural difference.

Developmental Model of Intercultural Sensitivity

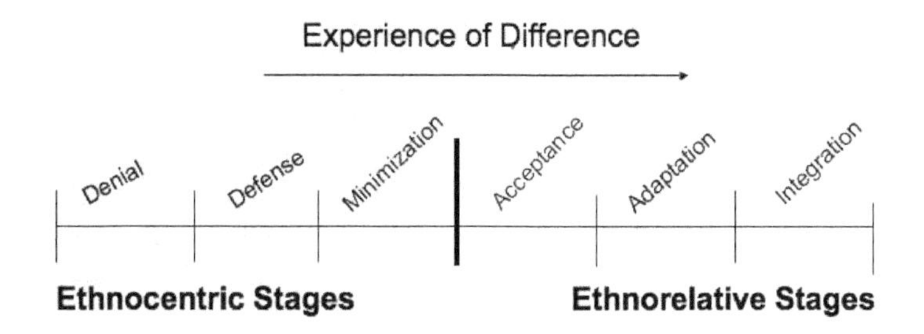

The first three are ethnocentric, meaning events and behaviors are interpreted from one's own cultural viewpoint. One's culture is experienced as being central to reality. The last three are categorized in the ethnorelative phase, where one's own culture is experienced in the context of other cultures.

The underlying assumption of the model is that as one's experience of cultural difference becomes more complex and sophisticated, one's competence in intercultural relations increases. It goes on to state that changes in cognitive structure are directly related to an evolution in attitudes and behavior toward cultural difference.

The Ethnocentric Stages

Denial is the most basic stage of ethnocentrism, where one's culture is experienced as the only real one. People essentially assume there are no real differences among people from other countries. Cultural difference is either not experienced at all, or it is felt as a kind of non-articulated something. Although they might be a witness to a tremendous number of foreign cultural experiences, they generally fail to make something out of them. There is no successive construing and reconstruing of what happens.

As in the story Little Red Riding Hood, *people in denial actively refuse to "see" cultural differences.*

An example is the experience of American students, who have just come back home after a one-week stay in Munich. When asked about their experiences in the Bavarian city, they answered that it was "just like home". Upon further inquiry, their reply was, "Well, Munich has lots of buildings, too many cars and McDonald's." This statement demonstrates an *active refusal* to "see" cultural differences.

People in denial don't perceive changes at all, or if they do, it's in vague categories such as "foreigner" or "people of color". They stereotype others based on knowing only one or two things about the others. For example, some Europeans seem to think that all Texans wear cowboy hats and boots or Americans seem to believe that French men wear berets. These simplistic stereotypes make "their" seemingly limited experience appear less real than "our" rich experience.

Another extreme aspect of people in denial is that they sometimes unconsciously view people from other cultures as having less than human status. This form of dehumanizing can easily lead to the exploitation of others, such as child labor or forced prostitution, or in the extreme case, genocide. The massacre of the Armenians, the Jews in the Holocaust and just recently the arbitrary execution of Muslims in the former Yugoslavia, are just a few examples.

"Make it thy business to know thyself, which is the most difficult lesson in the world."

— Miguel De Cervantes

In the next stage, ***defense,*** one's own culture is experienced as superior, the only good one and all others are viewed as inferior, "underdeveloped". People perceive cultural differences; however these differences from the norm are labeled negatively. They are considered a threat to one's self-esteem and identity.

This derogatory attitude toward difference is generally called "negative stereotyping," — undesirable characteristics are attributed to every member of a distinct group. The extreme form of defense is found in persons who have become members of neo-Nazi groups or the Ku Klux Klan. A more typical common defensive statement might come from a European, who, after a frustrating two-month stay in the USA, comes to the conclusion: "Americans are superficial and uncultivated."

Some people may enter into a reverse form of defense. Long-term sojourners, such as Peace Corps volunteers in Peru, may put down their own culture and become fanatic supporters of the adopted culture. They reject their American roots and idealize the simplicity of South American rural life. We say "they have gone native".

The DMIS predicts that as time goes by, people can move from defense into the ***minimization*** stage. As the term suggests, people at this stage minimize trivialize cultural differences. "With minimization, there's more recognition that we're dealing with people that are different, but there's still resistance to that idea," Bennett explains. "The belief is that somehow if we are more open in making sure that equal opportunity exists, everyone should be grateful and follow a set of rules. This assumption of similarity is then invoked to avoid the difficult work of recognizing one's own cultural patterns, understanding others, and eventually making necessary adaptations."

For instance, Americans may believe that everyone wishes for individual freedom, openness, and that "all people want to be successful". Or that religious people believe that "We are all children of God". Members of a dominant cultural group are usually unaware of how they may be perceived as privileged or culturally imperialistic by those from non-dominant cultural groups.

People in such a stage are excessively respectful of other cultures and seek to

People in the minimization stage see themselves as benevolent and open as in this gravue of the 17th century bourgeoisie, drawn brilliantly by Gustave Doré. Yet, in their "politically correct" mode, they unconsciously seek to impose their cultural values, which they sincerely believe to be universal.

avoid stereotypes by treating others as an individual or by treating other people as they would like to be treated. They are "politically correct". But deep down, they're still ethnocentric by holding unconsciously on to their culture-bound universalistic notions. As a result, they mistakenly believe "their" cultural values to be universal and hope that others will all converge into their cultural position, reflected by statements such as "Why can't they just be like us?"

This is currently the case in Eastern Europe where West European and American entrepreneurs want to introduce (in reality, impose) Western business methods. They are polite and respectful and see themselves as benevolent and open. Yet, they're perceived by the local population as insensitive, patronizing and imperialistic.

The Ethnorelative Stages

Acceptance is the first of the three ethnorelative stages. Here, there's a fundamental shift in the mindset from the unconscious assumption that one's culture is the definer of reality to a more conscious assumption that one's own culture is just one of many equally complex worldviews. People at the acceptance stage are at ease with ambiguity and understand clearly that there is no one right answer.

> "When you reach real ability, you will be able to become one with the enemy. Entering his heart you will see that he is not your enemy after all."
> –TSUJI (Japanese sword master)

Acceptance does not mean agreement — cultural difference may be judged negatively, but the judgment is not ethnocentric. There's an acceptance of deep cultural differences in communication, non-verbal behavior and thinking styles, with the insight that their ideas, feelings and behavior are just as rich as there own. People are curious about other cultures and seek opportunities to learn more about them. An example is the statement of a young Russian man, deeply in love with a Brazilian: "I want to learn Portuguese and everything about Brazil so that I can understand my Maria better."

Because there's an openness to all, people in this stage tend to avoid exercise of power in any form. If a cultural dilemma presents itself, there may be a paralysis of action posed by conflicting cultural norms.

The second ethnorelative stage, ***adaptation***, involves a more proactive effort when dealing with cultural diversity and the use of intercultural skills. The goal is to maximize relationships with people from other cultures.

In the adaptation stage, people make a more proactive effort in dealing with cultural diversity as evoked symbolically in Michelangelo's painting of The Last Judgment.

People in adaptation are able to look at the world "through different eyes", or as psychologists call it by "cognitive frame-shifting". It is a form of empathy that allows a temporary shift in perspective for the purpose of understanding or evaluating situations in either their own or the other culture. For instance, an Indian manager may routinely use his frame-shifting ability to act as a "bridge" between the French and Indians for conflict resolution. This means he or she intentionally changes their behavior to enhance communication.

If the person is a long-term expatriate, he or she may be bicultural — the worldview contains two fairly complete cultural frames. So, a French person, having lived in New Dehli for five years, might say: "I'm beginning to feel like a member of this culture."

The final ethnorelative stage is ***integration***. One's experience of self is expanded to include moving in and out of different cultural worldviews. People at this point don't think in ethnocentric terms at all but are comfortable with multiple and ambiguous cultural conditions.

Such a person is capable of seeing and feeling the relativity of beliefs — there is no absolute standard of "rightness". This ability to see one's self within a collection of various cultural frames of references can cause some to lose their primary cultural identity and create what might be described as internal cultural shock. The subsequent breakdown of identity leads to *cultural marginality* — existing on the periphery of two or more cultures.

This stage is not necessarily better than adaptation, but it is common among long-term expatriates and "global nomads". Despite the periodic confusion in identity, people in the integration stage often say, "I truly enjoy participating fully in these varieties of cultures."

THE UNBEARABLE LIGHTNESS OF BEING INTERCULTURAL

Once the sixth stage of integration has been attained, one can be described as interculturally competent. But what are the characteristics?

To begin with, watch for complex allegiance. An intercultural person has gone beyond an original group's value-system and is able to adapt. Identity becomes less fixed, more a process than a product. The experience of self moves in and out of different worldviews, and people no longer think in ethnocentric terms — as in, "my country is the best." They are comfortable with multiple and ambiguous cultural conditions and become, in a sense, "cross-cultural swingers," juggling of two or more competing value-systems.

> "Wisdom is not wisdom when it is derived from books alone."
> — HORACE

A good example of this is Arnold Schwarzenegger: when he visits Austria, he's as Austrian as you can get, but upon returning to California, he swings back to his adopted American-ness. Whatever the reader thinks of him as an actor or politician, he demonstrates nonetheless intellectual and emotional openness to others, the ability to embrace the change necessary for growth and the freedom to be different.

In the vast majority of cases, the intercultural person speaks more than one language. Through language you learn not only vocabulary and grammar, but an entire way of understanding the world, a set of frames in which experience and meaning are connected. And each new linguistic reality teaches you much more about yourself.

The intercultural person is able to understand and feel the relativity of values and decision-making, enhanced through multiple frames of references. It's a dynamic process, a continuing awareness of your own cultural boundaries, but parallel to that, allowing yourself to expand and wander into another person's mind. This "other" perspective, what we call empathy, permits events to be reconstructed as alternative cultural experiences.

However, this ability to see one's self within a collection of various cultural frames of references — a sort of "dynamic in-between-ness" — can lead to a breakdown of identity. It's at this stage when Milan Kundera's "unbearable lightness of being" takes on meaning. It suggests that each life is ultimately insignificant; thus, each decision one takes, whether based on your own culture or an adopted culture, ultimately doesn't matter; these decisions have no weight, they're "light," they don't tie us down.

But at the same time, insignificance is unbearable: when our decisions, i.e. our lives or "being" so not matter, we no longer exist. This condition is prevalent among long-term expatriates. Because of conflicting identities, they subconsciously tend to seek out other cultural marginals rather than people from any one of the cultures they know.

Despite the "unbearable" meaninglessness of an un-rooted life, people at this stage may seek out roles that allow them to be intercultural mediators, as reflected in statements like: "I love the varieties of cultures! Change is so stimulating, and keeps me from going stale."

Broadly speaking, this is a person who can understand and reconcile the dilemmas of the human condition, generating respect and appreciation for other realities. For example, when an American has decided to undertake a project on a trial-and-error basis, but is confronted with the Austrian need to plan everything out, the intercultural person will try to understand this need as a real — not a frivolous — concern and act accordingly.

This is not to say that the person has lost a sense of values. One always preserves some "ethnocentrism," certain fundamental habits of mind along with the "other-culture awareness." This is perfectly natural; a person needs a healthy identity-based ego and tested approaches to life. However, we are being forced to move from the "nationalistic" toward a greater recognition and acceptance of other ways of living.

But as we can never know another culture fully, the goal is to raise our sensitivity and reach some degree of cross-cultural comprehension.

IV

Global

Global Synergies

Managing Multi-Cultural Teams

WHY ARE GLOBAL TEAMS SO DIFFICULT TO MANAGE?

Nancy Adler, a world expert in group dynamics, writes in her book *International Dimensions of Organizational Behavior* that culturally diverse teams often perform below expectations. Managers' most common reaction to cultural diversity is simply not to acknowledge it or believe that it doesn't have an impact on organizations. This is a parochial attitude — viewing the world solely through one's own eyes and perspective. The second most common response is that managers behave in an ethnocentric manner — they perceive diversity, but see it as a source of problems.

Taking another perspective, Dr. Adler states that performance losses in multi-national teams can be traced back to diverse thinking patterns, disagreement on expectations and what information is considered relevant. All these factors lead to higher levels of stress than found in homogeneous teams.

Furthermore, members of multi-national teams demonstrate higher levels of mistrust due to the misinterpretation of different cultural behaviors and assumptions. For instance, Japanese team members are less likely to look other team members straight in the eyes, a behavior some European and North American managers may misinterpret as a lack of trustworthiness. At the end of the day Japanese colleagues may be delegated to trivial responsibilities.

Lastly, team members often stereotype others from less affluent countries negatively rather than objectively accessing their skills and potential contributions. Austrian bankers may assume their Romanian colleagues to be less competent simply because Romania is not as advanced technologically and economically as Austria.

Advantages of Multinational Teams

Dr. Adler points out that a well-led global team has the potential for superior productivity, especially in the creation of new ideas and synergetic solutions. Multi-cultural teams come from diverse backgrounds and don't feel the need to fit into the dominant presiding cultural norm. They're apt to create more alternative plans and solutions to problems than a homogeneous team.

Additionally, there is less groupthink. This occurs when team members, in their striving for unanimity, override their motivation to realistically appraise alternative courses of action. The consequences of groupthink are failure to examine the risks involved in the group's choice, incomplete weighing of alternatives and a failure to work out contingency plans. Obviously, if there's less groupthink, you're more likely to obtain different and original ideas and solutions.

Strategy for Developing Culturally Diverse Teams

To exploit the advantages of mixed teams and create synergy, managers need to take more time and effort by adopting certain measures. In examining the development of high-performing multicultural teams, Dr. Adler found the following qualities:

1. *Recognizing differences*: Research indicates that intercultural communication breakdowns are largely caused by ignorance of national differences. To overcome the natural ethnocentric perceptions, team members should first observe and objectively describe each cultural behavior without either interpreting or evaluating. At the same time, team members need to become acutely conscious of their own stereotypes and how they could inadvertently affect their expectations of fellow teams members from other cultures. This sort of reflection forces team members to understand why members from other cultures think, behave and feel the way they do. By doing this, members find out to their surprise that they are able to ask each other in a more objective fashion how they can contribute and complement the work of others.

2. *Cultivate openness:* The resourceful team leader will attach great importance to the cultivation of an open attitude toward cultural diversity. Team members should be encouraged to communicate their cultural values and explain reasons why they act the way they do. This permits other members to gain insight into the motivation and assumptions of the others. Furthermore, at the beginning the team leader needs to openly say that cultural diversity shouldn't be seen as a burden, but rather as an enriching, positive resource.

3. *Creating mutual respect:* For any multi-cultural team to work effectively, an atmosphere of mutual respect must be present. Team leaders can improve this by selecting members of equal ability and by informing the team of the prior accomplishments of each member.

4. *Equal power:* Two or more heads are better than one. This common sense axiom tells us productivity is higher if all team members participate. However, if too much power is accorded to members of one culture, it could lead to counter-productive activities, in that non-dominant team members could feel intimidated. The sensitive team leader should be careful not to vest too much power in his/her own ethnic group and strive to distribute tasks according to each person's ability.

5. *Establishing a vision and overriding goal:* Multi-national teams often have more difficulty in establishing their purpose and tasks than homogenous teams due to different assumptions and miscommunication. Right from the start, the astute leader will have the team articulate their vision or goal in such a super-ordinate way that it transcends individual differences. This, in turn, will provide general direction, decrease prejudice and increase mutual respect.

6. *External feedback:* Given the diverse cultural standards, multi-national teams have a harder time than homogenous groups in deciding collectively on what is a good or bad suggestion or decision. To prevent a breakdown in the team's effectiveness, there needs to be continual positive feedback in the initial phase. Even better is when an outside senior manager praises the team's progress and output. This can only solidify the team's unity. Team members learn to value contributions made by each member and trust collective decisions.

"Most ignorance is vincible ignorance: We don't know because we don't want to know."

– ALDOUS HUXLEY

MISUNDERSTANDINGS IN A GERMAN-AMERICAN TEAM

In 1995, German psychologist Sylvia Schroll-Machl examined the reasons American-German projects often fail. A German multinational brought her in to evaluate how American and German engineers and researchers interacted. It became clear early on that problems were due, in large part, to misunderstanding each other's way of problem-solving.

Schroll-Machl noticed that, at the outset of a project, Germans showed a greater need for detailed information and discussion. They tended to see the process from an engineering point of view, considering all of the difficulties that might arise, planning hypothetical solutions. The goal was to make sure everything would be done correctly, every element possible kept "under control". Avoiding uncertainty means avoiding anxiety.

The Germans expected all team members to share knowledge by sketching out their previous experiences. Reaching a consensus (which, they argued, permits the rapid implementation of any strategy) was essential. Schroll-Machl concluded that German decision-making concentrated on identifying problems, their history and components. Less emphasis was placed on results.

The action-oriented Americans found these discussions trying, often outright boring. The exchange of too much information felt like a waste of time, "paralysis through analysis". No matter how good a plan is, the thinking goes, it will be modified along the way. The Americans didn't speak up at this stage; by not saying anything, they hoped to speed up the process and get down to work. In their minds, problem-solving started out with a short brainstorming session to define goals and establish a series of approximate milestones.

Efficiency and creativity were the watchwords. The Americans wanted to "keep all options open", perceiving any project as a trial-and-error process. Schroll-Machl found their decision-making to be more open-ended, concentrating on a mission, a vision.

The Germans felt the Americans were acting without fully understanding the problem: "Shoot first and ask questions later." The Americans felt obsession with plans, and sticking to them, meant being locked into a rigid pattern, with no flexibility during the implementation-phase.

Once a plan was established, German team members were able to work relatively independently. Americans expected further group meetings and informal communication throughout. The Germans complained that the Americans asked about issues which had already been discussed at length.

Basic philosophies—"going on a mission" vs "minding the shop"—were only part of the equation, though. Americans are often given tasks for which they have not been thoroughly trained. Frequent job-rotation leads to a learn-by-doing attitude. It goes without saying that one communicates more with superiors, as well as other team members. Germans are, on the whole, better trained. Mechanics, machinists and the like go through the famous "Dualsystem" but even engineers and executives receive a holistic mix of the practical and the theoretical.

And, of course, the rules for doing business in Europe are stricter: whether it's cars, cosmetics or cold cuts, there are norms, guidelines, documentation which one actually has to read.

Germans also assume decisions made at group meetings are binding. Americans see them as guidelines which change when the need arises or a better solution presents itself. And Americans expect these changes to take place; it's part of the adventure!

Leadership, not unexpectedly, was also a major factor. The German leader is both an expert and a mediator (expected to convince, not order) who tends to vote with the group. During the implementation phase, there's little interaction with individual group members. "Distant" and "difficult to reach out to" was the way the Americans put it. The American leader defines goals, makes decisions, distributes tasks and makes sure they're done. Motivation and coaching are part of the chain-of-command style. Communication is intense by European standards and continues in a "baseball team" atmosphere all the way through completion and out for celebratory drinks afterward.

Schroll-Machl's study makes clear that if these differences are explained at the beginning, i.e. through intercultural training, chances for success increase enormously. However, if cultural awareness is not made a priority and the different communication styles are not understood, German-American projects often fail, causing both financial loss and hurt feelings.

Negotiating Across Cultures

An International Negotiation Failure

> A sales manager for a U.S. technology company was meeting the purchasing manager of one of Finland's leading corporations. He wanted to sell them a new product for the production line. Since the product application was quite new, the sales manager was hoping to get a premium for their technological innovation.

> The talk went well, and the Finnish decision-maker appeared quite interested. He asked for the price. "We firmly believe that this product will increase your quality enormously. We'll be able to sell it to you at 24 dollars a piece", the American responded. The Finn listened politely and said nothing. "Look, we would very much like to sell it to you and my company will be able to go as low as 20 dollars." The Finn still didn't say anything. Twenty painful seconds later, the American gave in: "All right, my rock bottom price is $17 dollars." The Finn suddenly appeared confused but pleased. He was asking himself how he got such a great deal without ever saying a word.

This type of cross-cultural encounter happens again and again. The US manager hadn't realized that silence is an integral part of Finnish communication style. In American "cultural language", silence usually signals a negative response. Because the American manager had not done his cultural homework beforehand, he arrived poorly armed when it came to interpreting non-verbal signals.

Cultural Influences on the Negotiation Process

As companies increasingly seek opportunities outside their national borders, executives often find themselves confronted with negotiating styles that go by different rules.

Every player in the game plays according to his or her own conception of bargaining. The following examples demonstrate the wide range of approaches in getting a deal.

In Japan and South Korea, the seller is hierarchically subservient to the buyer. A sales person is expected to provide whatever information and service the buyer requests. In return, the buyer is culturally expected to make sure the seller gets a profit from the business. This process stems from the Japanese notion of *Amae* — indulgent dependence — whereby the group higher in hierarchy is expected to take care of the lower party.

In US business culture there's a more egalitarian, competitive spirit, and each party goes into the negotiation with the attitude "may the best person win." Buyers and sellers are expected to take care of themselves by getting the best deal for their company. If Japanese and Americans are not aware of these differences, the results are too frequently irritation, anger and sometimes a negotiation collapse.

China, South Korea and other parts of Asia are consensus and status cultures. A handshake is often more important than a signed contract, An overly legalistic agreement may be perceived as a lack of trust. But even if a written commitment is worked out, many Western companies have found out the hard way that signing a contract may still not end negotiations. A contract is considered as a "snapshot in time" and is always open to renewed negotiation as circumstances change.

When negotiating with the Chinese

(a) practice patience; (b) accept prolonged periods of no movement; (c) control against exaggerated expectations, and discount Chinese rhetoric about future prospects; (d) expect that the Chinese will try to influence by shaming; (e) resist the temptation to believe that difficulties may have been caused by one's own mistakes; and (f) try to understand Chinese cultural traits, but never believe that a foreigner can practice them better than the Chinese.

Source: Lucian Pye, *Chinese Commercial Negotiating Style*

In efforts to build up the relationship, American negotiators often make many small concessions during the bargaining process, expecting their counterparts to reciprocate. Russians and Chinese don't feel compelled to behave in a similar fashion and may view the concession-giving as a sign of weakness, gleefully taking it without giving anything in return. They may even try to extort further "free" concessions.

These cross-cultural interactions illustrate how trusting our ability to "correctly" interpret the counterpart's behavior can ruin negotiation strategies and goals. In the same vein, situational and tactical factors can impact the bargaining process.

Situational and Tactical Factors

Location: It is usually advantageous to conduct the negotiations at your home office or a neutral location. Meeting at somebody else's workplace can be a disadvantage because it reduces access to information and increases travel-related stress and cost.

Physical arrangements: Sitting face-to-face, the traditional approach, is ironically not the ideal seating arrangement as it maximizes competition. Sitting at right angles facilitates more cooperation and synergy.

Number of participants: Americans are strong individualists and tend to believe in the "lone cowboy" manner of doing things. Bringing along extra team members for a negotiation is just an additional expense. Many forget however, that cross-cultural communication is complex and difficult. Giving someone the task of observing the non-verbal messages while the others conduct the negotiations has proven to be an effective strategy. Additionally, a group has the advantage of communicating more power and importance.

Status difference: Most people in the world respect formality and distance and feel comfortable in a structured situation. Stating at the beginning that you wish to be on a first name basis and acting in an informal manner may make your counterpart uneasy. In almost all international encounters, conventional dress, correct vocabulary and style facilitate a more successful negotiation.

Face saving: Studies have shown that better negotiation agreements are obtained if there is a "moderate" adaptation to the other party's cultural patterns.

This is especially true when it comes to face saving. If you've been raised in a low-context environment and are dealing with people that place great value on relationships and indirect communication, your tendency to defend different positions with open disagreement and public confrontation may be perceived as highly insulting. The result may be "losing face" for both parties.

Time limitations: When negotiating overseas, don't ever mention your flight arrangements. Your Brazilian or Chinese hosts may be particularly charming in pretending to help you "reconfirm your travel plans"; what they really want to find out is how much time you have planned for the negotiation. Knowing your exact travel schedule can be used to play with your patience and squeeze out concessions at the last moment.

How a culture values time can impact the duration of a negotiation. The most cited example is the Paris Peace Talks designed to negotiate an end to the Vietnam war. The fast-paced American delegation at first rented a hotel suite for two weeks. The Vietnamese negotiators leased a chateau for one year. To their chagrin, the impatient Americans found they had to continually renew their weekly hotel reservations to accommodate the more relaxed Vietnamese. Seasoned negotiators always consider that negotiations may take longer than expected.

Additionally, consider the length of time devoted to social conversation to create a friendly, businesslike climate. Americans are task-oriented and tend to focus more on getting the contract signed quickly than developing meaningful relationships. This can be a disadvantage when dealing with South Americans, Asians, and Mediterranean Europeans; people in such cultures invest more time in collective talk at the start of a negotiation.

Asking many questions: Effective negotiators in any culture analyze the situation in terms of their own and their counterparts' needs, goals and underlying cultural values. This is done simply by asking many questions. As one famous and highly successful U.S. negotiator for athletes and film stars said: "I never learned anything while I was talking. I always learn when someone else was talking."

Studies of Japanese and Brazilian negotiators during the questioning phase found that Brazilians tended to ask fewer questions and offer their proposal more quickly than to the Japanese. However, it was the Japanese who always finished

Penn's Treaty with the Indians *by the American painter Benjamin West portrays the British colonist William Penn negotiating the purchase of land with the Lenni Lenape Indians, more commonly known as the Delaware tribe. William Penn was an astute negotiator, paying much attention to cultural factors and the need to develop mutual respect. He acquired land through fair business practices rather than conquest, and by doing so, cemented an amicable relationship between Quakers and Indians that lasted for almost 100 years. The French philosopher Voltaire praised this "Great Treaty" and wrote, "It was the only treaty between those people [Europeans and Indians] that was not ratified by an oath, and that was never broken."*

earlier in the agreement phase and were more satisfied. The moral of the study was simple: the more questions you ask, the more likely you are to have a quick and successful negotiation.

Language comprehension: Another aspect to consider is the use and comprehension of English as a foreign language. The possibility of half-understandings is very high and could result in an unnecessary breakdown of the meeting. It's important to check if your perceptions are in line with the other party's. It is best to ask:

"If I understand you correctly, you say that..."

and then summarize what you think you've agreed on. Only by continually checking the other party's intention can you build up good business relations. Good communication creates confidence and reduces the probability of misunderstandings.

Qualities of a good negotiator

What then are the characteristics of a good negotiator that distinguishes that person from the average one? To a large extent, it depends on whom you ask. Some cultures, such as the American and Brazilian, stress the need for good verbal skills and rational thinking. Others, such as Japanese, put more emphasis on interpersonal skills, stressing both verbal expressiveness and listening ability. To the Chinese, the successful negotiator is an interesting person who exhibits persistence and determination. These differences reflect the diverse ways in which people view negotiations.

Research into successful negotiations shows, however, that good negotiators tend to use the following tactics and strategies:

Planning phase

- Explore as many options and alternatives as possible.
- Focus not only on the short-term, but also on the long-term.
- Seek to establish common ground in areas of conflict.
- Set range limits for more bargaining flexibility.

Exploring and bargaining phases

- Have high expectations and make high initial offers (or requests).
- Ask a large number of questions as a primary source of information.
- Refrain from making many commitments until the final stage of negotiation.
- Tend to avoid disagreement and agree with their partners as much as possible.

- Use active listening both to check whether they have understood and to summarize what they think has been agreed on.
- Use fewer arguments — strong arguments lose their power when diluted with too many weak arguments.
- Carefully observe the other side's non-verbal communication and are aware of their own.
- Work continuously to develop personal relationships and mutual respect.
- Use fewer irritators that cause annoyance, e.g. "This is a very fair price", "We are making an extremely generous offer".
- Make fewer defend/attack spirals.
- Use fewer counterproposals; rather clarify their understanding of counterparts' suggestions before responding with their own proposals.
- Make more behavioral labels, e.g. "Can I make a suggestion?", "May I ask a question?" to forewarn counterparts.
- Make more "feeling" commentaries, e.g. "I would like to accept this, but there is a part in me that feels unsure. Can you help me resolve this?"

In international negotiations, the most important characteristics of a *global negotiator* are:

- being aware of the cultural factors at play (intercultural competence)
- good listening skills
- an orientation toward people
- a willingness to use team assistance
- high self-esteem and an attractive personality
- high aspirations
- patience
- credibility and influence at the home organization

When all is said and done, you'll have a considerable psychological and tactical advantage when you are willing to change and adapt your behavior to your counterpart's expectations. You'll become more tolerant, be open to change and more importantly, there will be far fewer misunderstandings.

Intercultural Quiz

Evaluating Your Intercultural Competence

Take this quiz and measure how much you know — or don't know — about your intercultural knowledge and skills. For each statement, choose an option that is closest to your experience and thought. If your answer is "never", write 1; if it is "always", write 4, etc. Tally and rate your score with the answer key on page 136.

Options

1	Never
2	Occasionally
3	Frequently
4	Always

1. When I am in a new country, I try to learn some of its history, geography, manners, etc.
2. I look forward to having new intercultural experiences.
3. I identify and compare basic cultural differences and similarities with my own and other cultures.
4. Although I may not always understand why people in the other culture behave differently, I seek to understand their internal logic.
5. I enjoy acting as a cultural bridge between people from different cultures.
6. When meeting somebody from another culture, I assume difference until similarity is proven.
7. I can change my behavior to adapt to the other culture's norms.
8. I reflect on situations in my own culture based on my practical knowledge and facts of other cultures.
9. I use my skills and foreign experiences to help reconcile potentially difficult cross-cultural situations.
10. When in an intercultural situation, I can see my own and other cultures from an outsider's and insider's perspective.
11. I interpret values and behaviors from a variety of frames of reference so that there is never only one possible way of viewing things.

12. I try to see the connection between language and cultural behavior.
13. I'm aware that my culture is neither inferior nor superior to other cultures.
14. When communicating interculturally, I check if my perceptions are in line with the other party by asking "If I understand you correctly, you say that..."
15. I think of culture as the collective programming of the mind.
16. I recognize that so-called primitive societies also have highly developed and complex minds.
17. I am conscious of my own ethnocentric tendencies and work towards keeping them in check.
18. Before participating in an international negotiation, I anticipate the effect of cultural differences.
19. I analyze an intercultural situation through the process of first observing and resisting immediate tendencies to interpret and evaluate.
20. I try to use cross-cultural conflicts to deepen my knowledge of myself and others.
21. I try to incorporate opposites into mutual, synergetic solutions.
22. I believe that the real aim in intercultural relations is not so much understanding foreign culture, but understanding our own.
23. I'm comfortable with the notion that there are no absolute right or wrong answers in intercultural relations.
24. In working in a cross-cultural setting, I actively seek to understand the other person's perspective.
25. I use my language not only for communicating, but also as a system of organizing my perceptions and thoughts.
26. I understand cultural misunderstandings more as a clash of differing realities.
27. I'm conscious how my mother tongue acts as a "conditioner" of reality, which can prevent me from considering new values or mental approaches.
28. I keep checking for shared understanding in intercultural situations.
29. I actively use stereotypes as an initial guide for understanding foreign behavior and, if need be, modify them when the actual experience proves it to be otherwise.
30. I find it stimulating to be in a situation where I have to question my own way of thinking and behaving.

Solution

Answer Key:

If you have chosen "always" for each statement, you'll have a perfect score of 120. A sum total between 90-120 indicates a competent and skilled international person. This doesn't mean you should stop learning; you can always deepen and improve your knowledge and skills.

If you marked 70-89, you have some catching up to do, but you are not committing too many intercultural faux-pas. You need, however, to develop your skills further.

A score below 69 strongly suggests that your skills are limited and that you need to hone your global competence considerably. Identify your weakest areas and try to understand why you didn't answer correctly. That alone is the first step to becoming interculturally competent.

ANSWERS TO EXERCISES

Exercises on pages 19, 25, 31, 37, 43, 43, 46 are partially adopted from *Culture Matters - The Peace Crops Cross-Cultural Workbook,* exercise on page 93 is partially adapted from *Developing Intercultural Awareness* by Robert Kohls and John Knight.

Page 19: Universal, Cultural, or Personal Exercise (suggested answers)

Universal behaviors: 4, 6, 10, 12, 15
Cultural behaviors: 3, 9, 13, 14
Personal behaviors: 1, 2, 5, 7, 8, 11

Page 25: Linking values and behaviors (suggested answers)

1. Directness — At a meeting, openly telling your boss he's wrong.
2. Importance of family — Taking time off from work to visit your mother in the hospital.
3. Fatalism — Submissively accepting that some events in life are predetermined.
4. Honesty — In court, telling the truth under oath.
5. Respect for age — Listening to an older person even though you're not interested.
6. Informality — Arriving at a meeting without a tie.
7. Respect for authority — Asking the engineer's opinion of something he's an expert on.
8. Indirectness — Expressing your disappointment through irony, satire.
9. Relying on only oneself — Refusing to help the student next to you during an exam.
10. Egalitarianism — Letting the interns give their opinions on sales figures.

Page 31: Theoretical Frameworks – Individualism vs. collectivism (suggested answers)

These behaviors are *more* commonly related to ***individualism.***

2. Bonuses are based on your individual performance, not who you are.
4. This promotes an individual.
5. Contracts remind people to stay honest; collectivist people just know that people will be honest (otherwise they will be excluded from the group).
6. There's no loyalty to the company.
7. Collectivists avoid conflicts because it destroys harmony.
8. To stand out means wanting to be different from others.
10. This encourages independence by making a decision for oneself.
11. The emphasis is on the self-initiative.
15. Collectivists provide for everyone and then expect to be provided for later on.

These behaviors are *more* common to ***collectivism***

1. This applies more to older people who are listened to and perpetuate customs.
3. Collectivists stay together to form a united front.
9. Saving face means harmony is preserved.
12. Every group feels equally respected.
13. The group, i.e. family feels more secure and happy.
14. Collectivists decide what is proper and correct for others to hear.

Page 37: UNCERTAINTY AVOIDANCE EXERCISE (suggested answers)

High uncertainty avoidance: 1, 3, 5, 7, 9, 10, 11, 15
Low uncertainty avoidance: 2, 4, 6, 8, 12, 13, 14

Page 43: DIRECT AND INDIRECT EXERCISE (suggested answers)

A possible order would be 3, 7, 1, 4, 5, 2, 6, 8. Also remember, the tone of voice can be determinant — the longer phrases could sound sarcastic and ironic and the shorter ones could be said extremely politely.

Page 43: HIGH- AND LOW-CONTEXT EXERCISE (suggested answers)

Indirect/high-context: 2, 5, 6, 8, 9, 10

Direct/low-context: 1,3, 4, 7

Page 46: MONOCHRONIC AND POLYCHRONIC EXERCISE (suggested answers)

Monochronic: 1, 5, 7, 11, 13, 15

Polychronic: 2, 3, 4, 6, 8, 9, 10, 12, 14

Page 86: HOW NON-AMERICANS PERCEIVE AMERICANS

Qualities most associated, in order of preference

1. energetic
2. industrious
3. inventive
4. friendly

Qualities least associated, in order of preference

1. lazy
2. sexy
3. honest
4. sophisticated

Page 93: DISCOVERING ETHNOCENTRISM (suggested changes)

The purpose of this exercise is not to discover whether the statements are valid or not, but to stimulate thinking on how pervasive ethnocentrism is and how difficult it is to form non-judgmental statements.

1. The fact that the first automobile was invented by Gottlieb Daimler is proof of the technological ***skill / capacity*** of Germans.
   Using the term 'superiority' implies that you think some cultures are better than others would foster negative cross-cultural communications.

2. Asians do many things ***differently.***
   No culture is inherently worse or better than others.

3. The ***international terrorists*** who flew jets into the World Trade Center ***valued their perceived beliefs above human life.***
   Using the word 'Arab' implies an ethnic group is responsible for the attacks.

4. ***So-called "primitive people"*** have reached ***different*** stages of civilization.
   Anthropologists have shown that 'simpler' forms of culture are just as sophisticated and complicated as those in post-industrial states.

5. ***Both minority and majority*** members of a population should ***respect*** each other.
   Mutual respect is a prerequisite to good intercultural relations.

6. Americans have ***a*** culture.
   Many Europeans falsely assume that 'culture' refers to the arts and refinements of the mind and feelings. However, if we accept the anthropological definition of culture, then every interacting group has one.

7. If other nations were as orderly and punctual as the Germans, the world would be a ***very different*** place and people everywhere would treat each other ***differently***.
   The word 'better' implies superiority, which again would foster poor intercultural relations.

8. English is the ***most widely used language in global business.***
   Saying English is the one unifying language is denying other linguistic realities.

List of Illustrations

Opposite the preface: *The Thinker* by Auguste Rodin, **Page 2**: Boots, **Page 7**: *Arearea* by Paul Gauguin, Neuschwanstein, Louis XIV, Statue of Liberty, *Matsuura Byobu* by Iwasa Matabei, Sphinx in Egypt, **Page 11**: *The Nightwatch* by Rembrandt, **Page12**: *The Breakfast* by François Boucher, **Page 16**: *Bambus* by Hsü Wei, **Page 20**: Iceberg, **Page 26**: *The Vitruvian Man* by Leonardo da Vinci, **Page 30**: John Wayne with permission from Batjac Productions **Page 58**: *Faces* by William Hogarth, **Page 63**: *The Tower of Babel* by Pieter Bruegel, **Page 65**: John F. Kennedy, **Page 66**: Mount Rushmore, **Page 69**: *Johann Wolfgang von Goethe* by Johann Tischbein, **Page 71**: Confucius and Lao-Tse by unknown painter, **Page 74**: Ch'en Hung-shou by T'ao Yüan-ming **Page 75:** *Jupitor beguiled by Juno* by James Barry, **Page 76**: British and French rivalry, English gravure of the late18th century, **Page 80**: Mark Twain, **Page 85:** *Mona Lisa* by Leonardo da Vinci, **Page 89**: National stereotypes, English gravure of the 18th century, **Page 95**: *Goldfish out of water* with permission from John Malley **Page 100**: *Odipus* by Jean-Léon Gérôme, **Page 103**: Prime Minister Nehru in the USA **Page 104**: French gravure of the early 19th century, **Page 109**: *Bonjour* by Gustave Courbet, **Page 112:** *Little Red Riding Hood* by Gustave Doré, **Page 114**: *The Doctors* by Gustave Doré, **Page 116**: *The Last Judgment* (excerpt) by Michelangelo, **Page 120:** *The Meeting* by Honoré Daumier, **Page 126:** *Infirmitiés* by Honoré Daumier, **Page 128:** *Yusa Buson* by unknown Chinese artist, **Page 131:** *Penn's Treaty with the Indians* by Benjamin West

Bibliography

Adler, N.J., *International Dimensions of Organizational Behavior - 4th Edition*, PWS-Kent, 2002

Bennett, M.J., "Towards Ethnorelativism: A Developmental Model of Intercultural Sensitivity", *Cross-Cultural Orientations*, University Press of America, 1986

Bennett, M.J., Overcoming the Golden Rule: Sympathy and Empathy, *Basic Concepts in Intercultural Communication: Selected Readings* (pp. 191-214), Intercultural Press, 1998

Bennett, M.J., *Intercultural Communication and the Construction of Intercultural Experience*, Seminar in Winterthur, Switzerland, May, 2006

Bryson, B., *Mother Tongue — The English Language*, Penguin Books, 1990

Daloz, L, Keen, C., Keen, J. Parks, S., *Common Fire: Lives of Commitment in a Complex World*, Beacon Press, 1996

Franesco, A.M. & Gold, B.A., *International Organizational Behavior*, Printice Hall, 1998

Gibson, R., *Intercultural Business Communication*, Oxford University Press, 2002

Griffin, R. & Pustay, M., *International Business - 4th Edition*, Pearson Education, 2005

Hall, E. T. & Hall, M.R., *Understanding Cultural Differences*, Intercultural Press, Inc., 1990

Hofstede, G., *Cultures and Organizations — Software of the Mind*, Profile Books Ltd., 2003

Kennedy, P., *The Rise and Fall of the Great Powers*, Random House, 1987

Koester, J. & Lustig, M., *Intercultural Competence — Interpersonal Communication across Cultures*, Longman, 1999

Kohls, L.R. & Knight, J.M., *Developing Intercultural Awareness*, Intercultural Press, Inc., 1994

Kohls, L.R., *Survival Kit for Overseas Living*, Intercultural Press, Inc., 1996

Lewis, R., *When Cultures Collide*, Nicholas Brealey Publishing, 2000

Nees, G., *Germany Unraveling an Enigma*, Intercultural Press, Inc., 2000

Roland, A., *In Search of Self in India and Japan*, Princeton University Press, 1991

Schmidt, P.L., *Understanding American and German Business Cultures*, Meridian World Press, 2007

Schroll-Machl, "Die Zusammenarbeit in internationalen Teams — Eine interkulturelle Herausforderung dargestellt am Beispiel USA-Deutschland" *Internationales Change Management*, Schäffer-Poeschel Verlag, 1995

Schroll-Machl, S., *Die Deutschen — Wir Deutsche*, Vandenhoeck & Ruprecht, 2002

Stewart, E.C. & Bennett, M.J., *American Cultural Patterns*, Intercultural Press, 1991

Stori, C., *Old World New World*, Intercultural Press, 2001

Trompenaars, F. & Hampden-Turner, C., *Riding the Waves of Culture*, Nicholas Brealey, 1997

Vlasic, B. & Stertz, B., *Taken for a ride: How Daimler-Benz drove off with Chrysler*, HarperCollins Publishers, 2000

Culture Matters - The Peace Corps Cross-Cultural Workbook, Peace Corps Information, 1997

Internet:

www.dialogin.com

www.intercultural.org/resources

Index

About the Author

Patrick Schmidt, an American by birth and education, originally went to Stuttgart for a week-end visit in the mid-seventies and ended up staying 20 years. Through his work as an English teacher for German executives, and then as editor-in-chief of two German corporate magazines, he became an intimate observer of modern German culture. Later he lived and worked extensively in Kuala Lumpur, Malaysia and Montreal, Canada, specializing in cross-cultural management. He's the author of the books *Understanding American and German Business Cultures (German edition: Die amerikanische und die deutsche Wirtschaftskultur im Vergleich*) and *Dancing to a Different Tune.* He currently advises global companies on intercultural business issues, providing training and coaching. He lives in Strasbourg, France.

E-mail address: patrick.schmidt49@gmail.com
Website: www.agcc.de

CPSIA information can be obtained
at www.ICGtesting.com
Printed in the USA
LVHW101721090921
697444LV00015B/1268